The
Earth book
for
Kids

An Introduction to Earth Science

Acknowledgments

Dan would like to thank his wife, Julie, for her unending love, support, and patience, and his friends, Emily Dix and Steve Turnbull, for their constant encouragement.

Disclaimer Kids should always be accompanied by an adult when outdoors, and it's your responsibility to recognize, and avoid, the potentially dangerous bugs, insects, plants, or animals in your area. Always be aware of the weather and your environmental surroundings, and stay off private property. Never collect anything unless you're certain you have permission to do so. Rock collecting is not allowed in national parks, on Native American reservations, and in most state and local parks. Collecting Native American artifacts is also illegal on public lands.

Edited by Brett Ortler

Cover and book design by Jonathan Norberg

Proofread by Dan Downing

Cover photos: **Islamic Footage/Shutterstock:** volcano; **Gaspar Janos/Shutterstock:** mountain landscape; **Ralf Lehmann/Shutterstock:** lava; and **Dan Lynch:** front (background texture, feldspar, granite), back (malachite, shark tooth), spine (copper)

All photos copyright by Dan R. Lynch unless otherwise noted.
NASA: 54; **NASA/JPL:** 127 (top); and **Mike Norton:** 60 (top).

credits continued on page 175

10 9 8 7 6 5 4 3 2 1
The Earth Book for Kids: An Introduction to Earth Science
Copyright © 2022 by Dan R. Lynch
Published by Adventure Publications, an imprint of AdventureKEEN
310 Garfield Street South
Cambridge, Minnesota 55008
(800) 678-7006
www.adventurepublications.net
All rights reserved
Printed in the United States of America
ISBN 978-1-64755-283-1 (pbk.); ISBN 978-1-64755-284-8 (ebook)

The Earth Book for Kids

An Introduction to Earth Science

Dan R. Lynch

Adventure Publications
Cambridge, Minnesota

Table of Contents

Introduction to Geoscience

The surface of the Earth is an exciting patchwork of soaring mountains, deep oceans, and vast plains and deserts. But as amazing as these places are, the science of how they formed is even more incredible! That's because as solid as the ground beneath our feet seems, the Earth is always changing. Inside the Earth, deep underground, it is very hot, and the rocks are soft and move slowly. Everything above them—including us and the ground we walk on—moves with those rocks!

And change is always happening on the surface, too. When it comes to geology, nothing lasts forever—rivers, mountains, and even entire continents move—and they will disappear someday. And by looking at the Earth today and how its continents and oceans fit together, we can figure out what the world looked

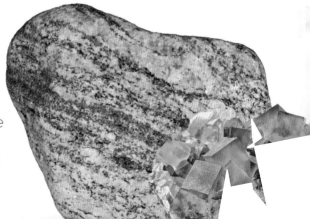

like long ago. We can even predict what the planet will look like in the future!

The study of how the Earth and its features form and change is called **geoscience**. Someone who works in geoscience is called a **geoscientist**. There are lots of different kinds of geosciences—some geoscientists study the atmosphere (the air), some study the hydrosphere (the water), and others study the biosphere (how plants and animals interact and evolve). In this book we're going to focus on **geology** (the study of rocks and how they can change) and the **lithosphere**, which is the hard outer layer of the Earth where we find all the mountains, lakes, plants, and animals.

The Earth is a special place, and incredible things happen deep beneath our feet, but you are probably wondering how it all works! We'll talk all about it in this book, but first we need to know: What is the Earth?

The Earth and What It's Made of

What do you think the Earth is made of? You might say that it's made of rocks. And that's true! But rocks are made of mixtures of special chemicals called minerals. When lots of minerals form together in the same space, they grow together to become a rock. But what are minerals made of? To answer that, we have to look a lot closer at the tiny particles that make up minerals and everything else in the universe, including you and me: atoms, elements, and molecules. In this chapter, we'll talk about all the little "building blocks" that make up our world!

What Is the Earth?

Earth is the third planet in our **Solar System**; the first four planets in our solar system are rocky planets; the outer four planets are gas giants (they have atmospheres of thick gas, but not much "ground" to speak of). So far, Earth is the only planet we know of that has life, like plants, animals, and humans. All the planets orbit the Sun, which means they spin around the Sun on an oval-shaped path.

The Sun

Our solar system. Earth is the third planet away from the Sun. The size comparisons between the planets are true to life, but in reality the planets are much farther apart.

Most of Earth is made up of rock, but depending on where in or on the Earth you look, the rocks can be very different. Rocks on the Earth's surface (the kind you can find and pick up) are cold, hard, and brittle, which means that even though they are very tough,

Minerals make up the Earth, and all of the rocks that we see have lots of minerals inside them. When they have enough room to grow, minerals form crystals, which are special shapes that minerals can make. These are crystals of quartz *(say it "kwarts")*, one of the most common minerals of all!

9

they can break. But many of the rocky areas inside the Earth are very hot—so hot that the rocks can be soft and will bend rather than break! The Earth gets hotter and hotter toward the center, and at the very middle is a core formed of solid metal. The Earth stays hot inside because its rocks are very good at holding in heat and also because gravity inside the Earth and radioactive minerals (special crystals that release energy) make new heat.

If we were able to cut open the Earth, we'd see that it is made of several **layers**. Some layers are hard and others are soft, but they all get hotter as they get closer to the middle of the planet. The layer most important to us is the **crust**, which is the very top layer, on the outside of the planet. It's the coldest and hardest layer. The crust is where all the rocks you've ever seen are found, and it's the layer we live on. But the other layers below it can affect and change how the crust looks—they can even make the crust break and move! We will discuss how all the layers interact later in this book.

The Earth's Layers

If we could cut into the Earth, we could see that it is made of layers.

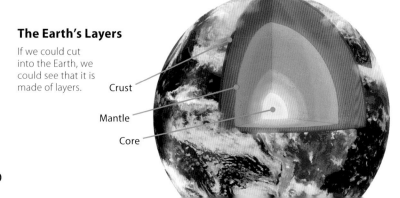

Crust

Mantle

Core

So now we know that the Earth is formed of rocks that are arranged into different layers, and that each layer is composed of different kinds of rocks. But what are rocks, and what are they made of?

This is a piece of granite, one of the most common rocks in the Earth's crust.

ROCKS AND MINERALS

Rocks and minerals are the materials that make up the Earth, and they can be found anywhere beneath your feet. But what's the difference between them?

Quartz *(say it "kwarts")* is a common mineral that forms pointed crystals. The purple kind of quartz is called amethyst *(say it "am-eh-thist.")*

A **mineral** is a special kind of hardened natural material. Minerals form when certain chemicals combine together and harden. For example, common table salt is actually a mineral called halite *(say it "hay-lite")*. Halite forms when two **elements** called *sodium* and *chlorine* combine together to make a chemical called *sodium chloride*. When sodium chloride hardens, it becomes halite.

A halite crystal

What makes minerals special is that when they harden, they form **crystals**, which have a special shape depending on the mineral. Halite forms crystals shaped like cubes, or blocks. (If you look at table salt through a magnifying glass, you may see little cubic crystals!)

Rocks are also hard, solid, natural materials, but they are made up of mixtures of minerals. Different kinds of rocks can have totally different mixtures of minerals in them. Some rocks have lots of different minerals in them while others have only a few. Sometimes the minerals in a rock are big enough to be seen as spots of color, but in other rocks they may be too small to see.

Rocks make up all of the landscape that we can see and are always underfoot. And even if you can't see rocks—say, in a

This is red granite, a type of rock. Each colored spot is a different mineral.

grassy park—that just means they're covered up. If you dig down deep enough, you'd eventually hit **bedrock**, which is the first layer of hard rock found below all the grass, loose dirt, soil, and mud.

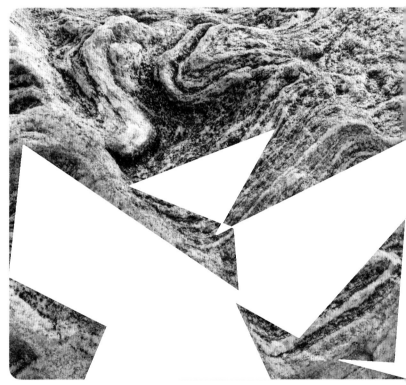

A lot of changes can happen to rocks as they get older. This rock, called gneiss *(say it "nice")*, got its wavy layers after being exposed to lots of heat and weight deep underground.

Minerals form inside rocks, both as *part* of the rock as well as in the spaces and cracks hidden in them. You can find minerals as the little spots of color that are stuck tightly in a rock, but if you're lucky, you'll also find nice mineral crystals hiding in a hole or crack in a rock. When they form inside a hole, they may be found on the walls of an opening, and you might be able to see their full crystal shape.

This is a rock. The red spots are a mineral called garnet, and the white areas are a mineral called quartz. They are formed tightly together in a solid piece, which makes it a rock. The garnet and the quartz are both parts of the rock.

The hole in this rock also contains garnet and quartz. The garnets are the little red crystals and the quartz is the white, glassy crystals. They're the same minerals as in the rock above, but they had more space to form, so we can better see their shapes!

To understand the difference between rocks and minerals, it's helpful (really!) to think of ice cream. Ice cream is made of different ingredients, like cream, sugar, and flavorings. Once the ingredients have been blended together to make ice cream, you couldn't separate them again without melting and ruining the ice cream. Minerals are the same way— the ingredients in them are elements, and you can't easily separate them.

Now, imagine that ice cream is a mineral, and that bananas, chocolate, and nuts are minerals, too. When you mix them together to make an ice cream sundae, that's a lot like different minerals forming together to make a rock! The sundae is like a rock because lots of distinct things combined to make it. But if you wanted to, you could pick out the nuts and still have a sundae.

Of course, a sundae isn't hard and solid like rocks and minerals are, but it is a tasty illustration of how many different parts can come together to make some-thing totally different!

WHAT MAKES A MINERAL?

Minerals are made up of certain chemicals that form naturally in the Earth. Chemicals are made of **elements**, which are special materials that are often called "building blocks" because everything is made up of combinations of elements, even you and me! You've probably already heard of many different elements; iron, copper, gold, oxygen, and helium are a few common examples. Elements are made up of **atoms**, which are so small that you need a very powerful microscope to see them. When atoms of different elements come together, they can **bond**, or attach, to each other. When atoms are bonded together in a group, it's called a **molecule** *(say it "mall-eh-cule")*. And when lots of the same molecule come together, they stick to each other and form a larger group. It's a lot like making a small snowball, then rolling it around in the snow to make more snow stick to it, making it larger.

Molecules are very tiny, but under a microscope we can see that each kind of molecule has a particular shape. When many molecules of a certain

These are crystals of quartz, sometimes called "rock crystal," which is one of the most common minerals.

kind come together and harden, they make a mineral, and the molecules' shapes determine what the hardened mineral will look like. This is how crystals form. A **crystal** is a hardened mineral that gets a special shape from the way its molecules have come together.

Here's an example of how it works, using the mineral quartz *(say it "kwarts")*:

Atoms (tiny particles) of different elements can come together and bond, or stick to each other. In this example, the blue atoms are the element oxygen, and the red atoms are the element silicon. These are the two elements that make up the mineral called quartz.

When oxygen and silicon come together, they bond in the shape of a little pyramid, with four oxygen atoms surrounding one silicon atom. They stick together like this because of each element's special traits. Once they have bonded together, they have become a **molecule**. Molecules of oxygen and silicon make a chemical called **silica**. (We can draw a pyramid around the silica molecules to make them easier to look at.)

When lots of silica molecules (shown here as little pyramids) come into contact with each other, they begin to bond and build upon each other like a snowball rolled in the snow. The clump of molecules grows bigger in all directions as more molecules join it. But molecules stick together in a very organized way. See how a pattern begins to form?

Eventually, when enough molecules have come together and hardened, they become a **crystal**. This illustration shows how a crystal shape can develop when enough molecules have bonded.

This is a quartz crystal viewed from above. See how it has the same six-sided shape as the group of silica molecules above? Even big quartz crystals will have a six-sided shape, all because of the way the tiny silica molecules within them came together.

Build Your Own Molecules and Crystals

Using toy blocks, you can learn a little about atoms and molecules and even build your own model crystals at home!

In this activity, we use toy blocks to show how atoms form crystals. Pretend that the blue blocks, red blocks, and white blocks are atoms of three different elements; each color represents different kinds of atoms.

Using these blocks, you can make a small shape with them. This is similar to how atoms bond together to make a molecule! Keep making the same exact shape until you have lots of the same molecules.

Real molecules will start to stick together, and they do so in certain patterns. So you can start putting your toy molecules together, being careful to attach them all the same way. After you've put several of them together, look at the

shapes they make. Can you see a pattern beginning to appear? This represents how real molecules stick together in a neatly organized way.

If you keep carefully building the same pattern and add your toy block molecules onto the top and sides of each other, you'll start to see a shape appear. See how this group of toy molecules is making a cube, or a blocky square shape? The molecules themselves aren't shaped like a cube, but when they all come together and build on each other, they start to make a cube. This is a lot like how crystals get their shapes!

This is a real crystal of pyrite (*say it "pie-rite"*), a mineral. Pyrite forms crystals that are shaped like perfect cubes! Pyrite molecules are so small that we can only see them with a powerful microscope. We know that a single pyrite molecule isn't cube-shaped at all, but when many come together, the special traits of their atoms cause them to bond in a blocky shape.

MOVING MOLECULES

Molecules and the atoms that comprise them are always moving. They have energy, and they don't just sit still. Even in rock-solid objects, atoms are vibrating and bouncing off each other all the time. But how much they move is often a matter of how hot they are. The hotter an atom or molecule is, the more it and its neighbors will move and bump each other. The colder they are, the more the stay in place. While molecules themselves are too tiny to see, you can still see how they move around by looking at water.

Water is a natural chemical. It consists of the elements called hydrogen and oxygen. At room temperature, water is a **liquid**, and its molecules are jumbled up and disorganized. There is also enough space between each molecule that they have room to move. So when you put your hand in a bucket of water, the jumbled up molecules are able to bounce around each other to make room for your hand.

As water heats up, its molecules move more and more. And when water gets hot enough, it boils, which means the molecules are moving and jumping around a lot! But boiling water also makes steam. Steam happens when water molecules become so energetic that they bounce away from their neighbors and leave lots of space between them—so much space that they begin to float away into the air. When this happens, we call it **gas**, and steam made from water is a gas.

When water becomes cold enough to freeze, its molecules can't move nearly as much, and they begin to settle down. When they are moving less, they can start to stick together. And when water molecules start to stick together, they do so in an organized way because of the special traits of their atoms. When the water molecules have frozen into place, we call it ice, and ice is a **solid**. And, believe it or not, ice is actually a mineral! It also has crystals. Have you ever taken a close look at a snowflake? Snow-flakes have six sides because of how water molecules bond to each other. That means that every snowflake is a water crystal!

But why is all this important when we talk about rocks and minerals? Well, because when rocks heat up or cool down, their molecules move in the same ways!

HOW AND WHERE MINERALS FORM

Now that you know that molecules move around more when they are hot and are able to bond together and form crystals when they cool down, you may be wondering how this happens in the Earth. Minerals can form in many different places and in many different ways, but many result from a similar process.

Hot mineral molecules are energetic and can become mixed in with other kinds of molecules. An example is when you mix table salt into hot water. (Remember that table salt is actually a mineral called halite.) When salt is put into hot water, its molecules spread out and mix in with the water, and the salt disappears. When something like a mineral disappears into water or another substance, that mineral has **dissolved** *(say it "dizz-olvd")*. Its molecules are still there, but they have become separated from each other. When table salt, or halite, dissolves into water, the mixture of salt and water is called a **solution** *(say it "soh-loo-shun")*.

When a solution containing mineral molecules cools off, the mineral molecules stop moving as fast, and they can start to bond together and form a crystal. This is called **precipitation** *(say it "pree-sip-it-ay-shun")* and you can see it at home by dissolving a few scoops of salt in a glass of hot water, then waiting a few days for the water to cool off and dry up. If you're patient, you'll see a crust of salt crystals at the bottom of the cup! They precipitated out of the solution of warm

The Dead Sea in Israel is so salty that when the water dries up, lots of salt crystals precipitate on the shore.

water and salt because the salt molecules were able to bond together as the water dried up.

When water inside the Earth is heated up by the hot areas underground, it can dissolve minerals in it. The water can then move around and soak into rocks, and after it cools off, it will leave crystals behind. But how does the hot water move?

When molecules heat up and move around a lot, they leave more space between them, and they spread out from each other. For example, if you have a jar full of liquid water and a same-sized jar full of hot steam, the jar of liquid contains many more water molecules than the jar of steam does. Because the jar of water has more molecules in it, we say that it is more dense than steam; steam is less dense than liquid water. Things that are more dense will sink below things that are less dense, so the hotter water gets, the more it will rise above cooler water. This means that hot water and especially steam will rise above cold water. When you mix hot and cold water, the hot water will rise to the top and the cold water will sink to the bottom. This is called convection *(say it "con-veck-shun")*.

Convection doesn't just happen with water! It happens in air, too. Have you ever been in a hot room and found that it was cooler down by the floor? That's because hot air rises (this is how hot air balloons float up). Convection also happens in the hot, soft rocks inside Earth! That means hot rocks actually float above cold rocks— we'll talk about this a lot more later on.

A lava lamp is a fun way to see convection working. When the "lava" inside is heated up, it rises to the top of the bottle, and when it cools down again, it sinks.

Inside the Earth, convection also makes hot water (often containing dissolved minerals) rise up and soak into the rocks above it. When the water cools off, it precipitates minerals and their crystals in the spaces inside the rock.

When warm water containing minerals rises up into the spaces in rocks, it can cool down and leave crystals behind. This illustration shows water partly filling a hole in a rock and precipitating crystals.

This group of crystals filled a hole in the rock when hot water containing dissolved minerals soaked into it, then dried up.

Not all minerals form in hot water. Some form in red-hot melted rocks! Deep in the Earth where it is very hot, some rocks melt and turn into a thick glowing liquid called **magma**. If magma gets pushed up to the Earth's surface where we can see it, then we call it **lava**. This super-hot melted rock contains tons of dissolved minerals, and when it cools, the minerals precipitate a lot like they do from water! In fact, there are so many dissolved minerals

in magma that when they precipitate, their crystals pack together tightly and form a hard, solid mass. Solid masses of different minerals are called **rocks**!

Minerals can form in other ways, too, but precipitation from water or magma is one of the most common ways.

Grow Your Own Crystals

To get a better idea of how hot water full of dissolved minerals can make crystals grow, you can actually grow your own at home!

- Alum in granular or powder form, about 1.5 cups

  Note for adults: Alum consisting of potassium aluminum sulfate is best for this activity (it should specify on the label). Also, be aware that this activity can stain pans and utensils.

- Water, 1.5 cups
- A 1-quart wide-mouth glass canning jar
- A small saucepan
- A stirring utensil
- A piece of string at least 5 or 6 inches long
- A pencil, dowel, or other short stick

Then, with an adult's help, carefully follow these steps:

1. Boil 1.5 cups of water in a saucepan

2. Carefully begin to add the alum powder one tablespoon at a time, stirring to dissolve the alum into the water. This makes a solution.

3. Keep adding alum until you've stirred in about 24 tablespoons. At this point, you will have oversaturated the water and you may see undissolved grains at the bottom of the pan.

4. Carefully pour the hot, alum-rich solution into the open jar.

5. Tie the string to the pencil and place it across the top of the jar, allowing the string to dangle into the solution. Center the string so that it is not touching the jar.

6. Wait 45–60 minutes for crystals to grow. Be careful not to shake or bump the jar as movement can disrupt crystal growth.

7. After 45–60 minutes, carefully lift the string to see what crystals have grown! You may find that one large crystal has grown, or maybe that several smaller ones formed along the string. The longer you leave the string in the water, the larger the crystals will grow. However, if you leave it too long, they may grow so large that they fill the bottom of the jar and you won't be able to get them out.

Let's look at the science happening: alum powder, like salt or sugar, will dissolve in cold water, but only a little. Cold water won't hold very much dissolved alum in it. But if you heat up the water, a lot more will dissolve in it. When the water starts to cool down, it can no longer hold the dissolved alum, which begins to clump together and harden. This is called precipitation, and as it precipitates, it starts to crystallize. The crystals form on the string because they can stick to the string better than they can to the jar.

SECONDARY MINERALS

Not all minerals form when they precipitate out of water or magma. Some minerals form when older minerals lose molecules. As older minerals are affected by weather, especially by rain and water, molecules can be separated from them. As water carries those molecules away, they can then bond with other, totally different molecules. New minerals can form as a result, and they can look completely different from the older mineral that provided the molecules! These are called **secondary minerals**, and they can form right on top of the older mineral or far away from it.

Copper is a good example. Copper is an element that forms naturally as a mineral. It is a reddish-orange metal. But when water and other chemicals carry away and change its molecules, lots of secondary minerals can form. And many of copper's secondary minerals are very colorful! If you've ever seen a copper penny with some blue or green crust on it, those are secondary minerals! Secondary minerals can form right on top of copper in nature, too, or inside the rocks around the copper.

This is a natural piece of copper. It doesn't look very coppery, does it? That's because it's coated in lots of secondary minerals. All of the blue, green, and dark reddish-brown spots are different minerals that grew on top of the copper.

Copper can produce many secondary minerals, and lots of them are colorful! Here are a few examples:

Copper

Chrysocolla

Malachite

Cuprite

COMMON AND IMPORTANT MINERALS

The minerals here are some of the most common ones on Earth, and all of them help form the makeup of many different kinds of rocks. You'll find these as mineral grains inside rocks:

Quartz *(say it "kwarts")*
Quartz is one of the most common minerals on Earth, and you can find it just about anywhere. It is very hard, white or clear, glassy, and forms six-sided crystals. It is most abundant as the little white spots in rocks like granite.

Feldspars *(say it "feld-spars")*
There are many different kinds of feldspar minerals, and they are all closely related. They are very common, especially in **igneous** (page 33) rocks. They often grow blocky, light-colored, opaque (not see-through) crystals, but they are most common as the tan or gray spots in rocks like granite.

Micas *(say it "my-kas")*
There are lots of different kinds of mica minerals, but all of them form as very thin, flaky crystals. Mica minerals are often very shiny, too, so if you ever find a speckly rock with lots of shiny "glitter" spots, those are usually mica minerals.

Amphiboles *(say it "am-feh-bowls")*
Amphibole minerals are a group of closely related minerals that are usually dark in color and often have a fibrous texture, almost like the texture of wood. Amphibole minerals are most often seen as the dark spots in light-colored rocks like granite.

Pyroxenes *(say it "pie-rock-seens")*
Pyroxene minerals are a group of minerals that are usually dark (often black) in color and have a glassy shine to them. They are most common as black shiny spots in dark rocks like gabbro.

Olivine *(say it "olive-een")*
Olivine is a glassy, green mineral that helps build dark-colored rocks like gabbro. It is pretty common inside rocks, but it is usually so small that you need a magnifying glass to find its grains.

Calcite *(say it "kal-site")*
Calcite is a very common mineral that is soft, glassy, translucent (it lets some light through it), and can form both as pointy crystals or as blocky crystals. It is common in sedimentary rocks like limestone.

WHAT'S IN A ROCK?

Rocks are made up of mixtures of different minerals all tightly packed together. Each kind of rock has a different mixture of minerals in it, and if the mixture changes, it becomes a different type of rock. Some rocks are **coarse grained**, which means that they have lots of colored spots and speckles that you can easily see. In coarse-grained rocks, each spot of color is a mineral grain that grew to a large size, and each different-colored grain is a different mineral. Granite is a good example. But other rocks are **fine grained**, which means that their minerals didn't grow very large at all. Some fine-grained rocks have mineral grains so small that you can't easily see them, and the rock will look like it is a solid color without colored spots.

This colorful rock is red granite. Each different colored spot is a different mineral. Here are four of the main minerals in granite and what they look like when they form on their own as crystals.

Feldspar

Amphibole

Quartz

Mica

THE THREE MAIN TYPES OF ROCKS

Granite (felsic)

Gabbro (mafic)

Igneous rocks *(say it "ig-nee-us")* are rocks that formed from magma or lava (melted rocks) either deep inside the Earth or on the Earth's surface after a volcanic eruption. Igneous rocks that formed inside the Earth are called **intrusive**, and ones that formed on the surface are called **extrusive**. All igneous rocks come in two main types: **felsic** *(say it "fell-sick")*, which are usually light-colored, and **mafic** *(say it "may-fick")*, which are usually dark-colored.

Sandstone

Sedimentary rocks *(say it "sed-e-ment-air-ee")* are formed when little grains of material, like sand or mud, stick together and harden. This usually happens underwater in wide, flat formations called **beds**.

Gneiss

Metamorphic rocks *(say it "met-a-morf-ik")* formed when older rocks are squashed by lots of weight, heated by the hot Earth, or both. The heat and pressure can change the rock and turn it into a new type of rock. Metamorphic rocks can begin as igneous, sedimentary, or even other metamorphic rocks.

Inside Our Earth

Our planet Earth is an incredible place, and even though it is billions of years old, it's still changing! Earth has several layers, and the closer they get to the middle of the planet, the hotter the layers are. This means that deep below our feet, it is so hot that even solid rocks become soft and can even melt. And when the rocks are soft, all of the weight piled on top of them makes them move very slowly. These things are happening all the time, and they can make mountains grow taller, break huge rocks, and even move the continents around the world! From the crust to the core, in this chapter we'll talk all about what's inside our Earth.

Layers of the Earth

The Earth is made up of different layers, and each layer is hotter than the layer above it. The top layer, on the outside of the planet, is called the **crust**. The crust is the layer that all the plants, animals, and people you know live on top of. It is made up of cold, hard rocks. All of the mountains, valleys, plains, and other landforms you've ever seen are part of the crust. But the crust is thin (compared to the mantle and the core), and it is affected and changed by the layers of the Earth found below it.

The next layer down is called the **upper mantle**. Even though it's too deep to see, it's still one of the most important layers because it can cause lots of changes to the crust above it. It is divided into two parts: a warm, thinner upper layer called the **lithosphere** *(say it "lith-oh-sfeer")* and a hotter, thicker lower layer called the **asthenosphere** *(say it "as-theen-oh-sfeer")*. The lithosphere is hard and rigid and made of dense rocks. But the asthenosphere is so hot that the rocks there are soft and can move slowly when weight presses on them, a lot like warm candle wax. And just like water in a bathtub, hotter rocks in the asthenosphere rise upward and cooler rocks sink downward because of convection. This means that the asthenosphere is always moving and hot rock is rising.

The inside of Earth isn't just old, cold rock—it's hot and always moving! Volcanoes offer us a tiny glimpse inside our amazing planet, but there's a lot more going on beneath our feet!

Below the upper mantle is the **lower mantle**, which is very hot but is still hard and solid because it's too deep and the pressure is too great for rocks there to melt. And at the very center of the Earth is the **core**, which is composed mostly of iron! The core is divided into two parts: the **outer core**, which is so hot that the metal is in a molten liquid form that swirls around, and the **inner core** which is even hotter but is so deep and under so much pressure that it stays a solid ball of metal.

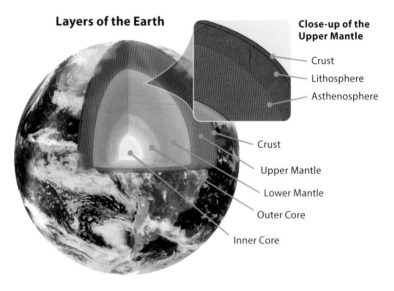

Layers of the Earth

Close-up of the Upper Mantle

Crust
Lithosphere
Asthenosphere

Crust
Upper Mantle
Lower Mantle
Outer Core
Inner Core

But how do all of these layers interact to make mountains and oceans? And why are some layers soft and some stay hard? Let's take a closer look at how the Earth's layers work.

INSIDE THE EARTH: HEAT AND PRESSURE

It is very hot inside the Earth—so hot that it can melt rocks!—but not all of the Earth's hot layers are soft. So why do the rocks in some hot layers get so soft that they can flow and move like hot wax while the rocks in other deeper layers are even hotter but stay solid?

We've all seen an ice cube or candle melt, but what is actually going on when that happens? When solid materials like rocks are heated, the molecules within them start to move more and more the hotter it gets (see page 20 to review how heat makes molecules move). Eventually the high heat makes the molecules move so much that they can't stick together anymore and they get very disorganized. This causes the rock to soften, which is called **melting**.

Pressure is the force that squeezes and crushes something when weight is put on top of it. If you have ever dived to the bottom of a swimming pool, you probably felt the weight of the water above you pushing on your body, especially in your ears—that feeling is the pressure of the water. The same thing happens inside the Earth, but millions of times stronger! The weight of the rocks in the crust and upper mantle is so heavy that they create very high pressure that squeezes and pushes down on all the layers below them.

Convection in the Kitchen

Hot liquids, like water and magma, have more energy than cold liquids. That means that hot liquids have a lot more space between their molecules than cold liquids do. This makes hot liquids less dense, so they rise above cold, denser liquids. This is called **convection**, and it happens inside the Earth with hot, soft rocks and magma. But hot water will rise, too, and with an adult's help, you can use it to see how convection works.

1. Fill a small Pyrex glass or measuring cup with water and add some blue food coloring. Stir until the water is dark blue, then put it in the refrigerator for an hour or two. (You could put it in the freezer to speed it up, but be careful not to let it freeze! Freezing could break the glass.)

2. After the blue water has chilled and is very cold, have an adult help you heat up a big glass container of hot water. (Adults: make sure to use a Pyrex bowl so that the high temperature doesn't

crack the glass.) Don't boil the water—it doesn't need to be that hot—but getting it very hot will help this activity work better.

3. Next, have an adult slowly and carefully tip the cold blue water into the container of hot water. Be careful not to pour it too quickly or splash it, otherwise  the water will mix up too much and you won't be able to see the convection happening.

4. Can you see how the cold blue water sinks right to the bottom of the bowl of hot water? Even though it's all just water, the cold water sinks below the lighter hot water.

5. After all the cold water has been slowly poured in, take a look: the bottom of the bowl will have more dark-blue cold water and the top will have more clear hot water.  Later, when the water is all the same temperature, the color will be more evenly mixed.

INSIDE THE EARTH: MAGMA AND LAVA

Most of the hot rock in the asthenosphere is soft, like warm wax. But when it rises to where there is less pressure, it can melt entirely, and it is called **molten rock**, which acts like a liquid. Molten rock that is deep inside the Earth is called **magma**, and it can stay hot for a very long time. Sometimes magma is pushed up through openings in the Earth's crust to where we can see it. These openings are called **volcanoes**, and some volcanoes are like tall mountains and others look like a crack in the ground. When magma is pushed out of a volcano, we call it an **eruption**, and when magma has been erupted onto the Earth's surface, then we call it **lava**. Lava cools very quickly when it is exposed to air; it quickly turns into solid rock.

While high heat usually makes the molecules in rocks move around, very high pressure can actually push on the molecules so hard that they stay locked in place. So even though the heat makes them want to wiggle around, they can't because the pressure is too high. That's why some layers of the Earth are still solid even though they are very hot!

We will be talking about magma, lava, and volcanoes all throughout this book, so remember what these terms mean!

Inside a volcano

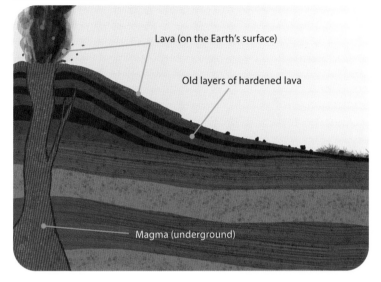

Lava (on the Earth's surface)

Old layers of hardened lava

Magma (underground)

The volcano in the photo below is in Iceland, and it erupted lots of lava onto the Earth's surface which quickly cooled to form black rock. Also, notice all the steam and gas coming out of the volcano, too.

Hot and Cold Rocks

To get an idea of how heat within the Earth can make rocks so hot that they become soft, try this:

1. Have an adult help you get some small blocks of wax. (Adults: blocks of paraffin wax are often sold in grocery stores alongside canning supplies.) Wax is a solid and is a little bit soft at room temperature. When  wax gets really hot, it can melt, and when it is really cold, it becomes very hard. This is a lot like how rocks can become softer or harder depending on how hot they are.

2. Place one block of wax in the freezer for a couple hours.

3. Place another block in a jar or bowl of hot tap water. You can place the wax in a plastic baggie to keep it dry, and then float the baggie in the hot water. Let the wax warm up in the hot water for 10–15 minutes.

4. Take the block of wax out of the freezer and feel how it compares to how it did when it was at room temperature. Does it feel harder? If you drop it, or gently hit it with a hammer, it will shatter because it has become harder and more brittle as it got colder. This is a lot like the cold, hard, brittle rocks you find on the Earth's surface.

5. Next, take the warmed wax out of the hot water and the plastic baggie and see how it feels compared to the cold wax. The warm wax will feel much softer and you may be able to push into it with your fingers. If you try to hit it with a hammer or drop it on the floor, the warm wax won't break but it will dent or deform. That's because it has become softer and less brittle as it warmed up. This is similar to what happens to rocks deep in the Earth; they have become hot, but they are under too much pressure to melt and become magma.

To see how high pressure can slowly change the shape and form of softened rocks, try this:

Cover the wax with a paper towel. Then put the warm wax on a hard, flat surface and balance a heavy, flat weight (like a stack of books) on top of it. Let it sit for a while until the wax cools. If the wax was warm enough, it will slowly begin to flatten. The wax is soft, but not melted, so the weight is able to compress it—just like rocks inside the Earth!

TECTONIC PLATES: HOW THE CONTINENTS MOVE

As solid as the ground may seem, the surface of the Earth (the crust) is always moving very slowly. But how? Remember that the lithosphere is the hard, top portion of the upper mantle (see page 36), and the Earth's crust sits on top of it. But the lithosphere is not one solid piece. It is broken up into several huge pieces that fit together like a giant puzzle. These pieces are called **tectonic plates** and they are always moving because of the hot, soft asthenosphere below them. In the asthenosphere, hot rock rises and cooler rock sinks, and that motion makes the tectonic plates above it move around slowly. Tectonic plates can bump into each other; some get pushed on top of others, some get forced below others, and some just slide past each other. And in all cases, the crust above them moves along with them. The places where plates meet each other are called plate **boundaries**, and it is along the boundaries where lots of changes in the Earth's crust happen, like where volcanoes form and earthquakes occur.

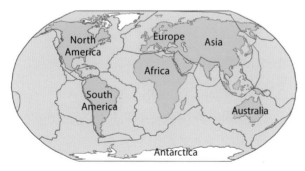

The red lines are the boundaries where the major tectonic plates meet.

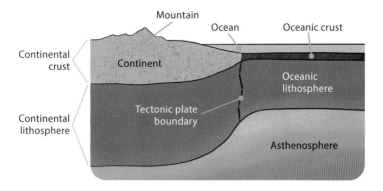

Mountain
Ocean
Oceanic crust
Continental crust
Continent
Oceanic lithosphere
Tectonic plate boundary
Continental lithosphere
Asthenosphere

THE DIFFERENT CRUSTS AND PLATES

Not all tectonic plates are the same. The thickest tectonic plates are found beneath the continents, so we call those the **continental lithosphere**, or continental plates. Between the chunks of continental lithosphere are areas of thinner lithosphere—those are found beneath the oceans, so they are called **oceanic lithosphere**, or oceanic plates. The **continents** are the big landmasses that make up our world, and they are only found on top of the thick continental lithosphere; they are made primarily of lighter weight felsic rocks, which we call **continental crust**. But the crust found at the bottom of the oceans, just above the oceanic lithosphere, is made of very dense, heavy, mafic rocks; we call it **oceanic crust**. The oceanic crust is very thin compared to the continental crust, but is actually heavier! All of these differences in thickness and weight of the lithosphere and crust means that they all move and interact differently.

TYPES OF TECTONIC PLATE MOVEMENT

The lithosphere is divided into sections called tectonic plates, and they sit on top of the hot asthenosphere. But the asthenosphere is thicker and denser than the lithosphere, which means the tectonic plates are actually floating on top of it. It's a lot like putting sprinkles on top of Jell-O—even though the gelatin is soft and the sprinkles are hard, the sprinkles won't sink into it on their own because they aren't dense or heavy enough. Since the heat of the asthenosphere keeps its hot soft rock moving around, the tectonic plates floating above it go along for the ride.

Tectonic plates can move in a variety of different ways, and a lot can happen at the plate boundaries where they meet, depending on how thick and heavy the plates are and which direction they're moving. Here we will look at the most common plate movements.

This is the San Andreas Fault in California as seen from an airplane. This long canyon is actually the boundary between two tectonic plates. These two plates are sliding past each other (transform movement) which makes earthquakes common here.

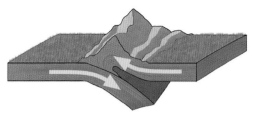

Convergent Movement (*Coming together*)

When two plates are pushed together, it is called a convergent movement. When two plates are pushed together, they can force rock upward to form a mountain range. If a continental plate and an oceanic plate come together, the heavier oceanic plate is forced downward into the Earth where it melts.

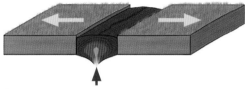

Divergent Movement (*Separating*)

When two plates spread apart and away from each other, it is called divergent movement. When two plates spread apart, mountains and valleys can form between them. At the bottoms of oceans, plates split and spread apart, allowing magma to rise and fill in the gap between them, which can make the ocean wider.

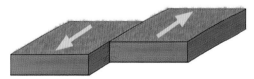

Transform Movement (*Sliding past*)

Sometimes two plates just slide past each other. As they do, they grind against each other, which can crack the rocks and shake the ground, which we call earthquakes. The movement can push up some rocks along the boundary, making small hills and valleys.

While it can vary, a tectonic plate usually moves around 0.4 to 2 inches (1 to 5 centimeters) each year. That doesn't sound like a lot, but it really adds up after a few million years!

EARTH THROUGH THE AGES: CONTINENTAL DRIFT

As the tectonic plates move, the crust on top of them moves with them. And since the continents are part of the crust, they move around, too. This means that the continents we know today were not always in the same place! By studying rocks and fossils across the world, scientists have been able to figure out how the continents have been connected together and how tectonic plate movements caused them to drift apart. This movement is called **continental drift**. The continents have been constantly moving for billions of years, but here we will look at how the Earth has changed since 425 million years ago, around the time when the first animals appeared on dry land.

425 Million Years Ago

Around 425 million years ago, the Earth looked very different. The oceans were larger and most dry land was south of the equator.

306 Million Years Ago

Around 306 million years ago, the continents started to clump together and drift farther north.

152 Million Years Ago

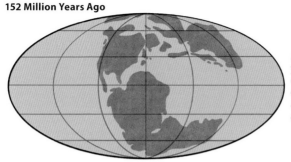

Around 152 million years ago, the continents had drifted farther north and started to break apart again.

94 Million Years Ago

Around 94 million years ago, the continents were starting to look more like the ones we recognize today, but they were still closer together.

Today

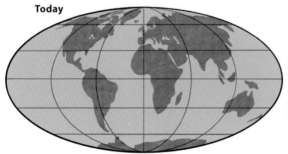

Today we have seven continents around the world, and the majority of dry land is on the northern half of Earth.

Stovetop Tectonics

Tectonic plates, the hot asthenosphere beneath them, and convection are all involved in how continents move and slowly drift around the world. A long time ago, all of the continents were connected together in one large supercontinent. But because of continental drift caused by the heat underneath the tectonic plates, that giant continent broke up and turned into several smaller continents. With an adult's help, you can recreate continental drift at home in the kitchen! This will show you how just rising heat can break up and move solid masses, like the tectonic plates. You'll need some heavy cardboard or thin sheets of wood (soft hobby wood, like balsa or basswood), a deep frying pan, some water, a stove, and an adult to help!

Measure the frying pan, then have an adult help you cut a circle out of the cardboard or wood that is about two inches smaller than the frying pan. For example, this is a 9-inch frying pan and the cardboard circle is 7 inches across. Then, have an adult carefully cut the cardboard or wood into several segments, like puzzle pieces. These pieces represent tectonic plates.

Fill the frying pan about one-third full of water, then carefully float your "tectonic plates" on the surface of the

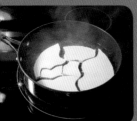

water, with no gaps between them. Now, have an adult turn on the stove to start heating the water. The water represents the soft, hot asthenosphere deep underground.

Watch carefully as the water heats up. Are any cracks appearing?

As the pan gets hotter, warm water will rise to the top of the pan and hit the underside of the plates, causing them to move. Watch how the cracks between each piece begin to widen! Some plates may try to move under or over others, too.

Eventually, some of the plates may drift off of the main group and completely separate themselves. Others may stay close to each other for a lot longer.

When the water has become very hot, all of the "tectonic plates" may separate. (Try not to let the water boil, as it may make the cardboard fall apart.) But even as they separate, can you see how they all would fit back together? Now, look at a map of the world and see if you can find any continents that also look like they would fit together.

Take a look at South America and Africa—does it look like they could fit together? That's because continental drift caused them to split apart millions of years ago!

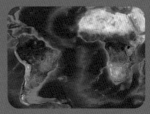

FAULTS AND EARTHQUAKES

The movement of the tectonic plates in the lithosphere carries the crust along with it, but the crust is made of cold, hard, brittle rocks. When tectonic plates move the crust, the rocks in the crust try to bend, but because they are so stiff, they eventually crack and break. The places where rocks break due to tectonic movement are called **faults**, and there are different kinds of faults that can form depending on how the tectonic plates in the region are moving. Faults can be easy to spot in nature because they can look like huge cracks that shift or offset the layered colors in rocks. Faults can continue to grow and get bigger as the tectonic plates below them keep moving.

When a new fault forms, or when an old fault gets larger, it can happen very suddenly. Big, sudden fault movements can shake the ground, making vibrations that can be so strong that they can make buildings fall down. This is called an **earthquake**. Near tectonic plate boundaries, earthquakes are very common, but most are so weak that they don't cause damage.

This cliff in Utah is faulted. You can clearly see how one side of the fault has slid downward, which broke the rock and offset the layered pattern.

These are the most common kinds of faults:

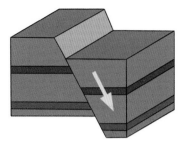

Normal Fault

In a normal fault, one side slips downward. This is often because the tectonic plates underneath the region are trying to spread apart, which causes the crust above them to stretch out.

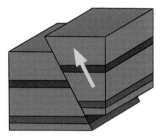

Reverse Fault

In a reverse fault, one side is forced upward above the other. This is often because the tectonic plates underneath the region are pushing together, causing the crust above them to crash together.

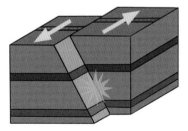

Strike-slip Fault

In a strike-slip fault, the two sides slip past each other; neither moves up or down. Both sides grind against each other as they slide. This kind of fault most often creates earthquakes.

Tectonic plate movements are so powerful that the faults they create can disrupt entire mountain ranges! This photo was taken from a satellite in space and shows a mountain range in China that has faulted so much that it looks like puzzle pieces that have slid apart! This powerful fault has shifted some of these mountains by up to a mile. The yellow and blue arrows point at rock layers that were once connected. The thin dotted line shows where the main fault is.

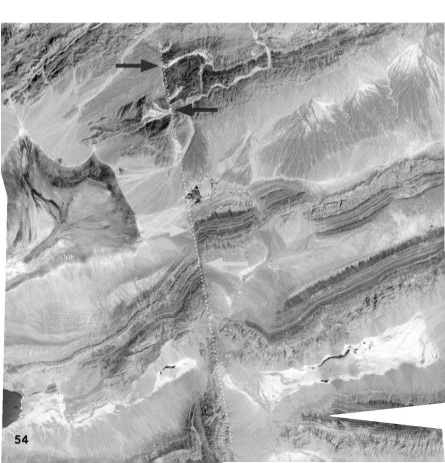

UPLIFT AND SUBSIDENCE

Tectonic plate movements can cause all kinds of changes to happen to the Earth's crust. Two of the most dramatic changes are uplift and subsidence. When two tectonic plates push into each other, one may be forced upward over

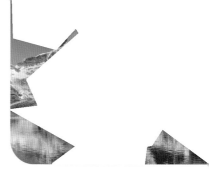

Two tectonic plates slowly pushed into each other to uplift rock and form the beautiful Swiss Alps mountain range.

the other. This is called **tectonic uplift** because the tectonic plate movements push up and lift the crust. Uplift can form tall, jagged mountains, but it can also make flat regions that are just a little higher than the areas around them, without any tall peaks.

When two tectonic plates spread apart, or when one drops below another, it can make the crust sink and form a low spot. When something sinks or drops, we

This photo was taken from one mountain looking across to another mountain, with a low valley in between. Tectonic subsidence formed the low spot.

say it subsided. So this is type of tectonic movement is called **tectonic subsidence**. Subsidence can make basins (low areas that can collect water) or valleys appear.

Potential Energy and Faulting

Faults are amazing examples of how the Earth's movements can crack and break solid rock. But it takes a lot of energy and power to fault a rock formation. So even though many of the Earth's rocks are always moving beneath our feet, and this creates pressure on other rocks, not all of them break, because not quite enough pressure has been put on them yet. For example, take some uncooked spaghetti noodles and bend them. You can bend them pretty far before they actually crack and break. When they are bent but not yet broken, we say they have **potential energy**, because your hands put energy into bending the noodles, and the bent noodles are holding that energy in them. When they finally break from being bent too far, the potential energy is released as the noodles snap! Rock faulting happens in a similar way—moving rocks, such as in the tectonic plates, can squeeze and bend other rocks, but they won't break or fault until pressed too far. But when enough potential energy builds up in them, they can suddenly crack and split!

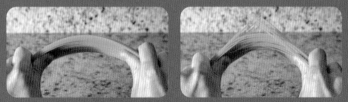

These bent pasta noodles have potential energy that is released once they're bent far enough to break.

Here's something else you can try: get some blocks—wooden blocks will work well. Plastic building blocks may be too small, but you can put several together to make larger square blocks. Next, put the blocks in a row and hold only the blocks at the ends with your hands. Then, push straight together on the blocks and lift them off the table. If you're careful, you'll be able to lift all the blocks off the table at the same time, even the ones you're not touching!

When you've lifted the blocks off the table just by holding the end blocks and pushing together on the rest of them, you've put potential energy into the row of blocks. As long as you keep pressing on them, they'll stay up.

If you release some of the potential energy by holding onto the blocks less tightly, the blocks in the middle of the row will fall. When movements in the Earth release pressure on rock formations, they can fall just like this, which causes faults to form.

If you increase the potential energy by pushing on the blocks even harder, some of the middle blocks will pop up out of place! When movements in the Earth increase pressure on rock formations, they can push rocks upward just like this, forming faults.

INTRUSIONS AND PLUTONS

When hot, soft rock from deep in the asthenosphere is pushed upward into the lithosphere, or even way up into the crust, we call it an **intrusion** *(say it "in-tru-shun")*, because it is intruding, or forcing its way,

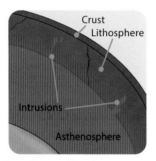

Intrusions are like blobs of melted rock that rise up through the lithosphere.

into the upper layers of the Earth. Intrusions are often like fingers or blobs of magma that rise upward toward the crust. If they reach the Earth's surface, they make a volcano. But most intrusions stay deep down where they cool off very slowly. But they can stay hot for so long that they start to change the older rocks around

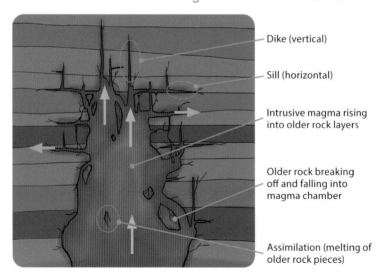

Dike (vertical)

Sill (horizontal)

Intrusive magma rising into older rock layers

Older rock breaking off and falling into magma chamber

Assimilation (melting of older rock pieces)

them. The hot **intrusive magma** can seep in between layers of older rock (called sills), or make new channels that rise upward through the rock (called dikes). It can also break off and melt pieces of older rock, which is called **assimilation** *(say it "a-sim-ill-a-shun")*.

Huge intrusions that stay deeply buried and slowly cool to turn into one huge block of coarse-grained rock are called **plutons**. We never see a pluton form because they do so deep in the Earth. Even after they cool, plutons usually stay hidden underground, but sometimes they be found on the Earth's surface where we can see them. But how does that happen?

Plutons are so solid that they can stay in one piece for a very long time. Sometimes tectonic uplift can eventually push them upward, but they can also be exposed, or revealed, when the rocks around them are weathered and worn away.

This is a mountain in California called Liberty Cap. It is a pluton that was exposed when all the rocks that used to surround it were weathered and worn away. Even though it's a high mountain peak today, it formed deep down inside the Earth!

DIKES AND SILLS

When intrusive magma rises up into older rocks, it doesn't always stay as one big blob. Sometimes it forces its way into cracks in the rock and hardens, making new rock features. A **sill** is when magma pushes sideways into the older rock around it and forces itself between the rock layers. This makes the older rock layers rise upward a little to make room for it. Sills form parallel (in the same direction) to the older rock layers. When you see a sill in real life, it can look like a thick layer of rock that doesn't match the rocks above and below it.

In this photo, you can clearly see a thick sill of intrusive rock that formed between the dark layers of sedimentary rock.

Sills form when intrusive magma forces its way between layers of older rocks. Sills form parallel (in the same direction) as the older rocks. This causes the older rock to bend and break upward to make room for the magma.

When magma pushes upward through older rock layers, it can form tall cracks that rise up through many layers in the rock. The older rock gets pushed out of the way, side-to-side, to make room for the rising magma. After the magma cools and hardens, it becomes a tall, thin rock formation called a **dike**. Dikes form perpendicular (in the opposite direction) to the older rock layers. When you see a dike in real life, it can look like a thick slab of rock that doesn't match the direction of the rock layers around it.

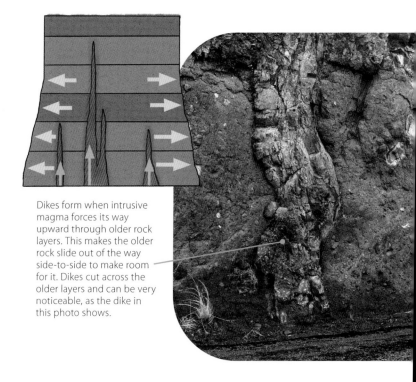

Dikes form when intrusive magma forces its way upward through older rock layers. This makes the older rock slide out of the way side-to-side to make room for it. Dikes cut across the older layers and can be very noticeable, as the dike in this photo shows.

TECTONIC PLATES AND RISING MAGMA: A SUMMARY

There's a lot to learn and remember about what happens deep inside the Earth. Review this illustration to remember some of the important things happening beneath your feet!

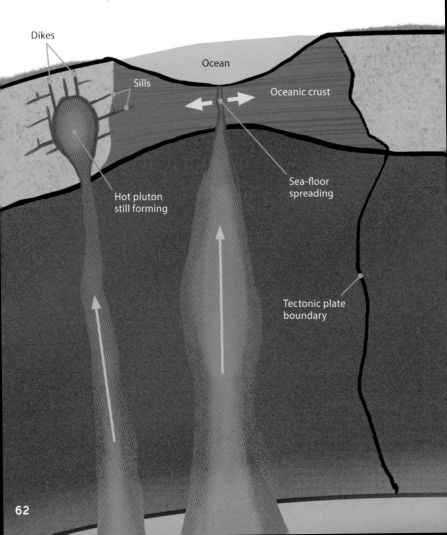

Dikes

Ocean

Sills

Oceanic crust

Sea-floor spreading

Hot pluton still forming

Tectonic plate boundary

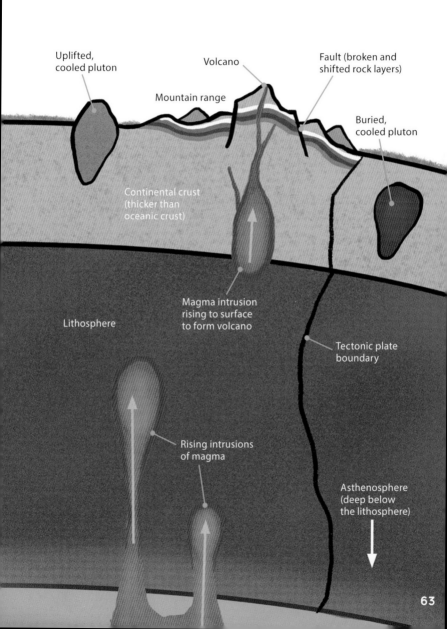

Uplifted, cooled pluton

Volcano

Fault (broken and shifted rock layers)

Mountain range

Buried, cooled pluton

Continental crust (thicker than oceanic crust)

Magma intrusion rising to surface to form volcano

Tectonic plate boundary

Lithosphere

Rising intrusions of magma

Asthenosphere (deep below the lithosphere)

Rocks

No matter where you go, you can always find rocks. Beneath our cities and forests and soil, layers of hard rock are always there because they make up the Earth's crust that we live on. But depending on where you look, you'll find very different kinds of rocks. If you're near mountains, you may find hard, glittery, speckly rocks, but if you're near the ocean, you may only find soft, crumbly rocks. The difference between them is because of how and where they formed. From deep within the hot Earth to the bottom of cold, calm seas, in this chapter we'll take a look at the different kinds of rocks and what makes each of them special.

These rocks are slowly being split apart by plants!

The Rock Cycle

The three main groups of rocks—igneous, sedimentary, and metamorphic—are all very different because they form in very different ways. And rocks are not permanent, either; an igneous rock today may become a metamorphic rock millions of years from now, or it could wear away into dust! The way rocks form and change from one kind into another is called the **rock cycle**, and it is happening all the time—it never stops!

Desert regions are some of the best places to see amazing formations and beautiful colors in rocks because there aren't many plants covering them up. Places like this make it easier to learn about rocks and how they get their amazing features, such as these layers of color.

The next page shows a diagram of how the rock cycle works, and how the three main kinds of rocks can change from one type into another. The arrows indicate the different kinds of natural forces that change the rocks. They are:

Weathering and **erosion**—When rain, wind, water, ice, and even plants break up rocks and wear them down into tiny pieces called **sediments**. Sand is an example of a sediment.

Heat and pressure—When rocks become buried, the weight above them squashes them with lots of pressure while the heat inside the Earth softens them. These forces can cause rocks to **metamorphose**, or change, into something new.

Melting—When rocks become so hot that they turn to liquid.

Cooling and hardening—When magma cools off and turns back into hard rock.

Compacting and hardening—When lots of little sediments are pressed together and begin to stick to each other, becoming a hard rock over time.

THE ROCK CYCLE

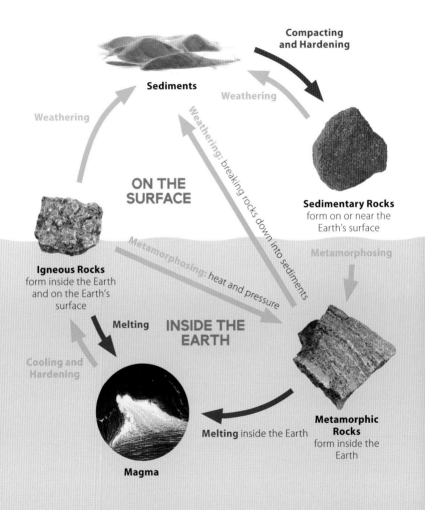

Compacting
and Hardening

Sediments

Weathering

Weathering

Weathering: breaking rocks down into sediments

ON THE
SURFACE

Sedimentary Rocks
form on or near the
Earth's surface

Metamorphosing

Metamorphosing: heat and pressure

Igneous Rocks
form inside the Earth
and on the Earth's
surface

Melting   INSIDE THE
EARTH

Cooling and
Hardening

Metamorphic
Rocks
form inside the
Earth

Melting inside the Earth

Magma

IGNEOUS ROCKS

Igneous rocks are some of the most important rocks to learn about because they make up most of the lithosphere beneath the crust. That means that igneous rocks are always somewhere below your feet! They form when soft, melted rock cools and hardens; igneous rocks can form from **magma** deep in the Earth or **lava** when it is on the Earth's surface. But what kind of igneous rock forms depends on which minerals are dissolved in the magma or lava, and on how fast the melted rock cools. Some igneous rocks are spotted and light-colored because they had a mixture of light-colored minerals and cooled very slowly. Others are dark and evenly colored because they had a mixture of dark-colored minerals and cooled very quickly.

Some examples of igneous rocks

COOLING AND CRYSTALLIZATION

When magma or lava cools off, the jumble of minerals in it begins to **crystallize**, or harden, to become crystals. Some minerals can form at higher temperatures, so they form first, when the magma or lava is still really hot. Other minerals can only form after the

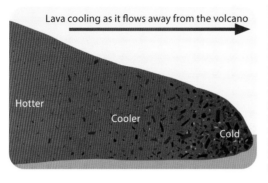

Lava cooling as it flows away from the volcano

Hotter
Cooler
Cold

When lava (melted rock) has erupted from a volcano onto the Earth's surface, it flows away from the volcano like thick syrup. As it flows away, it gets cooler. When the lava is still very hot, there are very few crystals in it. But as it cools off, more and more crystals form and begin to fit into each other like puzzle pieces.

melted rock has cooled down a lot, and they form last. But once the rock has totally cooled and hardened, all of the minerals in it have crystallized. The mineral crystals inside igneous rocks are tightly packed together—locked tight like puzzle pieces. Some igneous rocks also trap gases as they cool, which look like round bubbles in the hard rock.

INTRUSIVE AND EXTRUSIVE ROCKS

Igneous rocks form when melted rocks cool off and harden, which can happen hidden deep inside the Earth or on the Earth's surface where we can see it. The Earth is good at holding heat, so inside the Earth, rocks cool much more slowly. This lets the minerals inside them grow to larger sizes. These rocks are called **intrusive** igneous rocks, which is easy to remember because they form inside the Earth. Intrusive rocks are usually **coarse grained**, because the mineral spots in them are coarse and big enough to easily see.

When melted rocks are pushed out onto the Earth's surface, they cool very quickly in the cold air. They cool so fast that the minerals inside them don't have time to grow very large. These are called **extrusive** igneous rocks, which you can remember by thinking that they exited the Earth. Extrusive rocks are usually **fine grained**, because the mineral spots in them are very fine and too small to see without a microscope.

Both of the rocks below are made up of the same mixture of minerals. But one is intrusive and cooled slowly and the other is extrusive and cooled quickly, which made them differ in grain size.

Granite is an intrusive igneous rock that cooled very slowly, so the minerals in it had time to grow to large sizes that are easy to see as colored spots. We call this coarse grain.

Rhyolite is an extrusive igneous rock that cooled very quickly, so the minerals in it didn't have enough time to grow to a size we can see. It doesn't have the big colored spots that granite does. We call this fine grain.

TUFF

Tuff is a special igneous rock that forms when a volcano throws lots of hot dust and ash out onto the ground. The ash is so hot that it sticks together and forms a rock.

MAFIC OR FELSIC?

Intrusive and extrusive igneous rocks are also separated into two main categories based on the minerals they are made of. They are:

Mafic *(say it "maf-ick")* rocks are those that contain lots of minerals rich in the elements magnesium, iron, and calcium. These minerals are often dark-colored, so that means mafic rocks are also usually very dark in color. Mafic rocks are most common in and near the oceans.

Basalt is a common mafic rock, often found by oceans.

Felsic *(say it "fell-sick")* rocks are those that are made up primarily of the minerals feldspar and quartz, along with other minerals rich with the elements aluminum, sodium, and potassium. These minerals are often light-colored, so that means felsic rocks are also

Granite is one of the most common felsic rocks.

usually lighter in color. Felsic rocks are most common on continents, especially in mountains.

Some rocks can be **intermediate**, which means they contain a mix of mafic and felsic minerals. Mafic rocks are more dense than felsic rocks, which means a small amount of a mafic rock can weigh more than a larger amount of felsic rock.

This photo shows a piece of granite under a special microscope. Each colored shape is a mineral crystal. See how big some of them are? Those formed first when the magma cooled, and all the little ones formed later and had to fit around the big ones. But they are all tightly stuck together, just like the pieces of a puzzle!

COMMON AND IMPORTANT IGNEOUS ROCKS

Granite *(say it "gran-it")*
Granite is one of the most common rocks because it makes up most of the continental crust. It is a felsic intrusive rock that contains lots of minerals, such as feldspar and quartz.

Rhyolite *(say it "ri-oh-lite")*
Rhyolite is a felsic extrusive rock that has the same mineral mixture as granite, but it looks much different because it was erupted onto the Earth's surface. Some rhyolite has lots of air bubbles trapped in it.

Gabbro *(say it "gab-ro")*
Gabbro is a very dark-colored mafic intrusive rock. It formed deep in the Earth and is made up of lots of minerals that contain iron. It is most common around oceans or in mountainous areas.

Basalt *(say it "buh-salt")*

Basalt is a common, dark-colored mafic extrusive rock. It has the same mineral mixture as gabbro, but it has much smaller grains because it was erupted onto the Earth's surface.

Diorite *(say it "di-oh-rite")*

Diorite is an intermediate intrusive rock, which means it has big mineral grains that are a mixture between the light-colored minerals in granite and the dark-colored minerals in gabbro.

Andesite *(say it "an-deh-site")*

Andesite is an intermediate extrusive rock. It has a similar mineral mixture as diorite, but it was erupted onto the Earth's surface where it cooled more quickly. Andesite eruptions are often the most explosive kind of volcanic eruptions!

Syenite *(say it "si-en-ite")*

Syenite is an odd intrusive rock that can be felsic or intermediate. It looks a lot like granite, but it is rarer and contains very little quartz. That's interesting because quartz is a main ingredient in most felsic rocks.

Igneous Rocks Quiz

Using what you've learned about igneous rocks and the minerals that make them, do you think you can tell which rocks are mafic, felsic, or intermediate just by looking at them? How about which ones are intrusive or extrusive? Remember these important differences between them:

Mafic: Dark rocks with lots of dark-colored minerals

Felsic: Light-colored rocks with lots of glassy minerals

Intermediate: Usually grayish rocks that have an equal mix of light- and dark-colored minerals

Intrusive: Rocks that cooled deep inside the Earth and have large, chunky mineral grains that are easy to see

Extrusive: Rocks that cooled quickly on the Earth's surface and have very small, fine mineral grains that are harder to see

Now look at the pictures of these rocks and see if you can guess if they are mafic, felsic, or intermediate, and if they are intrusive or extrusive. Some of these types of rocks have been discussed in this book, but others will be new to you! Don't worry if you get some wrong; it can be tricky!

1. Gabbro
(say it "gab-ro")

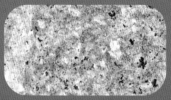

2. Andesite
(say it "an-deh-site")

3. Anorthosite
(say it "an-or-tho-site")

4. Granodiorite
(say it "gran-oh-di-oh-rite")

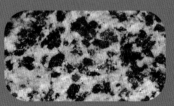

5. Basalt
(say it "buh-salt")

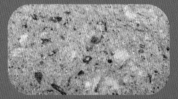

6. Trachyte
(say it "tra-kite")

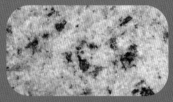

7. Diorite
(say it "di-oh-rite")

8. Rhyolite
(say it "ri-oh-lite")

Answers: 1. Mafic, intrusive; 2. Intermediate, extrusive; 3. Felsic, intrusive; 4. Felsic, intrusive; 5. Mafic, extrusive; 6. Felsic, extrusive; 7. Intermediate, intrusive; 8. Felsic, extrusive

Sedimentary Rocks

All rocks eventually break down over time. When wind, water, ice, plants, and other natural forces crack and break rocks, it can wear little pieces off of them. This is called **erosion**, and everything from whole mountains to little pebbles will break down into smaller pieces. Those little pieces are called **sediment**, and sediment comes in all different sizes, from pebbles to sand to tiny grains of mud or clay that you need a microscope to see! (We'll talk lots more about erosion later on.) Sedimentary rocks form when lots of sediment sticks together to form a new rock. Most sedimentary rocks formed at the bottoms of lakes, seas, and rivers, where lots of sediment sinks and forms thick layers called **beds**. Over time, beds of sediment can turn into hard sedimentary rocks when they are pressed by lots of weight, and when little bits of minerals get between the sediment grains and crystallize, kind of like glue!

Some examples of sedimentary rocks

TYPES OF SEDIMENT

There are lots of different kinds of sediment, and we organize the different kinds by their sizes. Big, coarse sediment like gravel can stick together to form different kinds of sedimentary rocks than small, fine sediments like silt. Let's take a look at some of the most common kinds of sediment:

Gravel is a kind of sediment that has big, coarse grains. Each piece of gravel is a small pebble that can be made of different kinds of rocks or minerals. Because each pebble of gravel is so big, it can be easy to figure out what kind of rock or mineral each pebble is made of.

Sand is a fine-grained sediment that has small grains. Sand is common on beaches, and you've probably felt how gritty and rough the little grains can be against your skin. Sand can be made of different kinds of worn-down rocks and minerals, but the most common mineral in sand is quartz.

Silt and **clay** are two kinds of sediments with very tiny grains—in fact, the grains in clay are so small you need a microscope to see them. But both kinds of sediments make sticky mud when they get wet. The grains of these sediments are so fine that they easily wash away, so these are mostly found in calm water, like at the bottom of ponds and lakes.

Not all sediments are made of worn-down, weathered rocks—some are made by animals! **Coral** consists of tiny sea animals that live in groups; each coral makes a hard shell around itself, and when lots of the shells grow together, they make a thick, hard mass. After many years, all of those hard coral shells can become compressed and hardened to form a sedimentary rock!

BEDS

Some layered cliffs can show different layers of sedimentary rocks. Each of these layers is a bed, and each formed from different sediments that gave them different colors.

HOW SEDIMENTARY ROCK BEDS FORM

Sedimentary rock beds often form at the bottom of bodies of water, like lakes or seas. When rivers wash sediment into lakes, it sinks and settles to the bottom and begins to build up into a layer, or bed.

Over time, different layers begin to build up. Changing seasons can cause different kinds of sediment to wash into the lake, making different-colored beds.

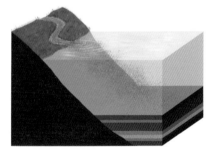

Eventually, the bottom layers will have so much weight on top of them that they press together tightly, locking the sediments together like puzzle pieces. This turns them into rock.

This layer of sand and mud is getting thicker and pressing down on the lower layers.

Sediment, like sand, sinks to the bottom of lakes or seas.

This sand doesn't have much weight above it, so it will stay as loose sand.

This portion of sand is under lots of weight pushing down on it, so it is hardening and turning into rock.

When weight presses down on a sediment bed, it can lock the sediments together. The sediments can also be "glued" together by tiny mineral crystals that form between the grains.

SEDIMENT ORGANIZATION

When a river or lake moves sediment around, the bigger, heavier sediment particles, like gravel, sink first, and the tiny, lightweight sediments sink last. When this happens, we say that the sediments have become **organized**, because the water has sorted them into layers by size. Neatly organized sediment beds turn into sedimentary rocks with grains of one size. But disorganized sediments form sedimentary rocks with differently sized grains in them.

The rock on the left is sandstone, and it is very organized—it has grains of all the same size. On the right is conglomerate, which is very disorganized—it has grains of different sizes.

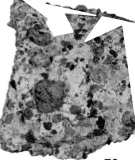

COMMON AND IMPORTANT SEDIMENTARY ROCKS

Sandstone
Sandstone is a gritty, rough rock formed when sand sticks together and hardens. Sometimes the grains are stuck so loosely that you can easily pick them off the rock. It forms at the bottoms of lakes or seas.

Shale
Shale is formed of many tightly pressed layers of mud and clay. It is a very soft rock, and many times you can even split apart the layers with your hands. It formed at the bottom of calm lakes and may have fossils in it.

Mudstone
Mudstone is similar to shale and is made of compacted mud and clay, but it is not layered because the layers were mixed up before they hardened.

Conglomerate *(say it "con-glom-er-it")*
Conglomerate is a poorly organized rock because it contains big pebbles mixed in with little grains of sand and clay. It formed in areas where fast moving water mixed up sediments.

Limestone *(say it "lime-stone")*

Limestone is a rock rich with calcite that most often formed from the remains of ancient coral reefs. The coral and other hard parts of sea creatures built up and turned into this soft rock. Some limestone can hold fossils inside.

Chert

Chert is a very hard rock that forms in different ways, but lots of chert formed when tons of tiny skeletons from microscopic sea life sank and built up at the bottoms of the ancient oceans.

Evaporite *(say it "ee-vap-or-ite")*

When salty ocean water dries up, it leaves layers of minerals behind that can turn into a soft rock called evaporite.

Travertine *(say it "trav-er-teen")*

Hot water from inside the Earth has lots of minerals dissolved in it. When it bubbles up to the surface at a hot spring, the minerals cool off and harden. Travertine is a rock that forms around hot springs when lots of minerals build up around the water.

Solidifying Sediments

Some sedimentary rocks, like sandstone, form when water soaks into the spaces between sediment grains and then dries up, leaving minerals behind. That happens because the water has minerals dissolved in it, and when those minerals precipitate, they fill up the tiny spaces between the sediment grains. When minerals form between grains of sediment, such as sand, it "glues" all the sediments together, turning it into a rock like sandstone! You can make your own sandstone by trying this:

You'll need some aluminum foil, sand, some white glue, some water, and a jar.

Find a bottle, dish, or other small object and then wrap aluminum foil tightly around it to make a cup shape with the foil. Then remove the object you wrapped the foil around. You should now have a cup-shaped piece of foil.

Next, carefully put some clean, dry sand into your foil cup. Fill it about halfway. (You'll want to do this in a tray or dish so that you don't spill sand all over!) This represents sand that has settled at the bottom of a lake or sea.

Next, put some white glue in a jar, then add a little bit of water. Stir it up well until it starts to look a little like milk. Don't add too much; just enough so the glue is runny.

Add the runny glue until no more soaks into the sand. (You'll also want to do this in a tray or pan in case the foil leaks.) Then carefully set it on a sunny windowsill or near a warm radiator and let it dry. It may take a long time to dry—sometimes weeks! But when it looks dry and feels hard, carefully unwrap the foil from the sand. See how the sand grains have now stuck together and hold their shape?

In real life, it isn't glue that holds sand grains together in sandstone, but minerals like calcite. Take a close-up look at your homemade "sandstone" (top) and compare it to real sandstone (bottom). See how similar it is?

Metamorphic Rocks

Metamorphic rocks form when older rocks are deeply buried and changed by heat and pressure within the Earth. The deeper a rock gets buried, the closer it gets to the hot interior of the Earth and the more weight piles up on top of it, putting it under tons of pressure that squashes it. These forces can change the rock, pressing its grains tighter and even making it so hot that it becomes soft and rearranges its minerals into layers. Sometimes a rock's minerals can even turn into new kinds of minerals, including precious gems. These changes are called **metamorphism**, and it can be so powerful that it can turn a rock into a completely new, different kind of rock! Igneous rocks, sedimentary rocks, and even older metamorphic rocks can be metamorphosed, or changed, into new metamorphic rocks. Some are formed just be heat, others just by pressure, but many are formed by the combination of both.

As this layer of rock becomes buried deeper, the weight from above and heat from below change it more.

Rocks higher up in the Earth press down on rocks below.

This layer of rock is being metamorphosed and changed into a new rock—it is being pressed by the rocks above it and heated from below.

Heat from deep in the Earth rises and softens the rock above it.

HIGH AND LOW GRADE

Metamorphic rocks that formed under low heat and pressure are called **low-grade** metamorphic rocks. Others that formed under very high heat and pressure are called **high-grade** rocks. Low-grade metamorphic rocks have changed a lot but can still look a bit like the original rock they formed from. But high-grade rocks have been changed so much that they look completely different, and may even have gemstones in them!

Many metamorphic rocks have a few things in common. The mineral grains in metamorphic rocks usually fit tightly together with no spaces between them. The minerals in metamorphic rocks are also often lined up in parallel layers, which means that the layers follow each other's shape but don't cross each other. And lots of metamorphic rocks have flaky, shiny minerals in them.

Low-grade metamorphic rocks can still resemble the rock they formed from. To the left is hornfels, a low-grade metamorphic rock that still looks a lot like the layered sedimentary rocks it formed from. On the right is eclogite, a high-grade metamorphic rock that was changed so much that it looks nothing like the dark gray igneous rocks it formed from.

FOLDING

The pressure that turns old rocks into metamorphic rocks doesn't always push downward; sometimes it can push from the sides. This can make metamorphic rocks that have been **folded**, which means that they have been bent or wrinkled. Folded metamorphic rocks can have wavy layers, sometimes zig-zagging back and forth, which shows that they saw a lot of side-to-side pressure when they formed.

CONTACT METAMORPHISM

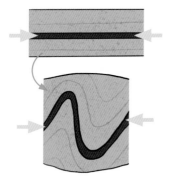

The yellow arrows represent the direction of the pressure coming from the sides, causing folding of the rock layers.

The layers of this metamorphic rock in England have been strongly folded back and forth.

Some metamorphic rocks form when intrusive magma touches older rock and "cooks" it. This is called **contact metamorphism**. The high heat of magma and steam can make the minerals in the older rock change into new minerals, creating new kinds of rock after it all cools and hardens.

When magma rises up into older rocks, we call it intrusive magma. Since magma is very hot and has lots of steam and other gases in it, it can change the older rock that it is rising up into. It does this by softening and heating the rock it touches. This can "cook" the older rock and turn it into a metamorphic rock.

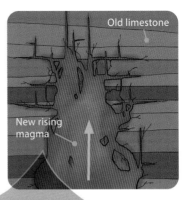

Old limestone

New rising magma

In this example, new magma has risen into layers of older limestone, which is a sedimentary rock.

Where the magma touches the limestone, it changes it into a metamorphic rock called skarn.

Later, when the magma cools, it will become granite, an igneous rock.

The magma's heat and steam go into the older rock.

Magma

Limestone: the older sedimentary rock that was already there

Skarn: the metamorphic rock that formed when the hot magma touched the limestone

Granite: the new igneous rock that will form when the rising magma cools off and hardens

COMMON AND IMPORTANT METAMORPHIC ROCKS

Schist *(say it "shist")*
Schist is a common metamorphic rock that forms mostly from sedimentary rocks like shale due to heat and pressure. Schist has lots of thin layers and is often flaky and glittery.

Gneiss *(say it "nice")*
Gneiss is a common metamorphic rock that forms when igneous or sedimentary rocks are exposed to very high heat and pressure. Gneiss often has lots of layers that can be wavy and have alternating light and dark colors.

Slate
Slate forms when shale is pressed and heated in the Earth. This makes the layers thinner, tighter, and harder. Slate is dark-colored, flaky, and brittle, and the layers can be carefully split apart.

Phyllite *(say it "fi-lite")*
Phyllite is a compact, layered rock that forms when slate is further metamorphosed under heat and pressure. This makes the minerals

in slate grow to bigger sizes, which gives phyllite a more glittery look.

Marble
Marble forms when limestone is metamorphosed by heat and pressure. It is often white in color and is made up of many tightly packed crystals of a mineral called calcite.

Hornfels *(say it "horn-fells")*
Hornfels is a tough, hard metamorphic rock that forms when magma touches and "bakes" older rocks. It can have a variety of different minerals in it, and while it may have layers, it doesn't break along them.

Quartzite *(say it "kwarts-ite")*
Quartzite is a rock that forms when sandstone is metamorphosed. It consists mostly of quartz. It is hard, tough, and a variety of colors.

Greenschist *(say it "green-shist")*
Also called greenstone, greenschist is a rock that formed when dark rocks like basalt are lightly heated and compressed. This turns its minerals green, making the whole rock green.

Metamorphism in Your Hands: Compression

Rocks deep inside the Earth are buried under so much weight that the pressure can completely change them. You can get an idea of the kinds of changes metamorphic rocks go through by using clay at home. Get two different colors of clay and make a few small, flat blocks of each color.

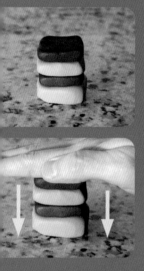

Stack the blocks of clay on top of each other so that you can easily see the different layers. Imagine that these are layers of sedimentary rocks like mudstone or shale.

Next, begin to press straight down on the stack of clay with your hand or something flat, like a book. Push straight down, but be careful, it may be difficult! This is called **compression**, and it happens when rocks are buried and all the weight above them presses down on them.

As you push down more and more, notice what happens: the clay layers mash together and get thinner and wider. Eventually, they'll be mashed so tightly together that you won't be able to separate the layers anymore. If this happened to real sedimentary

rocks, what do you think the pressure would do to them? It would change them into new kinds of rocks—metamorphic rocks—making them harder, more tightly layered, and might even change the minerals inside the rocks.

Sometimes the pressure on rocks does not come straight down on top of them. Sometimes the pressure comes from the sides. Now try pressing on both the sides of your clay layers. What happens?

The clay will start to fold upward or downward into a U-shape, or maybe a W-shape.

This is called **folding**.

If you look closely at metamorphic rocks in nature, especially around many mountain ranges, you'll find rocks with cool folds that look like waves. These formed by side-to-side compression, just like your clay example.

Metamorphism in Your Hands: Shearing

Many metamorphic rocks, like schist, have very thin layers of minerals within them, and sometimes they look glittery because they contain lots of little flat crystals of minerals called mica. These thin, tight layers can form when compression squashes the minerals, but it also happens by shearing. **Shearing** is a type of pressure that happens when part of the rock is pressed from one direction but the other part of the rock is not.

The diagram to the left shows layers of rock, and when they experience pressure only from the top-right side, the bottom of the rock formation stays put, but the top starts to shear to the left. This causes the rock to deform and stretch sideways.

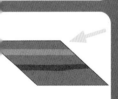

Try this: make a block of clay, then with a different color of clay, make lots of little dots and rice-shaped pieces. Then randomly press them into one side of the block so the little dots point in all directions. These represent crystals in a rock. Now begin to push on the block from

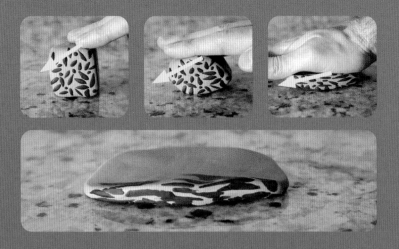

one of the top corners at a downward angle. Don't let the block slide as you push. You'll see the block leaning and getting stretched, but what is happening to the little "crystals"?

The block and the "crystals" will both get longer and flatter, and even though you placed the little dots of clay randomly, the shearing pressure will make them more lined up in the same direction. In nature, shearing can change the shape and order of real crystals in rocks the same way.

This is a photo of a real metamorphic rock called schist. You can see lots of very thin layers formed when shearing and compression changed the rock. How does it compare to your clay block?

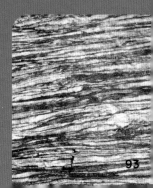

Rock Formations and Outcrops

The term "**rock formation**" can mean a few different things. Usually, a rock formation is a single body of rock. For example, a layer or cliff of sedimentary rock like sandstone can be called a rock formation.

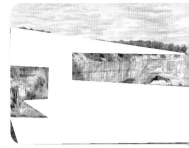

This cliff of sedimentary rock can be called a rock formation because it is all made of the same kind of rock and it all formed around the same time.

Other times, we may see a really neat rock outcrop with a strange shape or beautiful color and call it a rock

This huge, lonely rock can be called a rock formation because it is a unique outcrop formed when water and wind shaped and carved the rock.

formation. An **outcrop** is a spot where you can see solid rock on the Earth's surface, with no soil or plants covering it. Lots of times, outcrops with uniquely shaped rock formations are formed by weathering and erosion, which happens when things like rain and wind take little pieces of the rock away and naturally carve it. We'll talk a lot more about weathering and erosion later on.

So now you know that when you see the term "rock formation," you're reading about a specific layer of rock or a specific outcrop.

SOIL

In most places around the world, the very first layer of material beneath your feet is soil. **Soil** is a mixture of things and contains rotting plants such as leaves and wood, tiny living things like bacteria, often lots of water and gases, and also mineral particles. Soil is often soft and damp and makes a good home for plants to grow in.

Soil is a soft, damp material that has all of the things that plants need to grow. See how this plant's roots go deep into the soil?

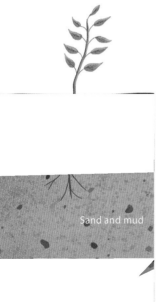

Sand and mud

Soil forms on the Earth's surface and covers up the rocks below it. When plants begin to grow in soil, their roots help keep the soil in place so that it doesn't wash away. In some places the layers of soil and sediments below it may be so thick that you would have to dig very deeply before you hit bedrock (the first layer of solid rock)!

This diagram shows how the soil and dirt on the Earth's surface have different layers determined by the size of their sediments. At the very top is soil, the damp, soft, rotten material that plants need to grow. And at the very bottom is solid, hard bedrock, the first layer of rock in the Earth's crust.

What's in Your Soil?

Soil is made up of differently sized sediments, like sand and silt, and you can easily find out how much of each is in the soil in your yard or park. Since different sediments have different weights—bigger sediments like gravel and sand are much heavier than tiny sediments like silt and clay—heavier sediments will sink much more quickly than lightweight ones. You can use this to see how much of each kind of sediment is in your soil. To try it out, you'll need:

- A large glass jar with a tight-fitting lid
- Water
- Dirt or soil from outside

1. Fill a jar about ⅔ full with water.
2. Put a few handfuls of dirt into the jar— be careful not to make the jar overflow.
3. Put the lid on the jar very tightly.
4. Shake the jar to mix up the dirt, then set it down and don't move it anymore. Watch what happens.

You'll see the heavy sand sink to the bottom very quickly, in just a few seconds.

Above the heavy, coarse sand at the bottom, you'll see another layer of finer sand start to settle in the next 30 seconds or so.

Let the jar sit for a while, and come back to it. After an hour, you'll see that some really fine-grained sediments have settled. That's silt, and it takes longer to settle than the sand because its particles are smaller and lighter.

After a full day, you'll see that the water will have gotten clearer, and another layer will have settled. The last layer is clay, and it is made of sediment so tiny that it takes a long time to sink and settle.

The layers you see when you try this will be different from the ones shown here. That's because not all dirt has the same mixture of sand, silt, and clay. If you use dirt from a forest or a garden for this experiment, it will most likely be a soil that will take longer to settle.

Bits of leaves and wood

Clay (thin tan layer)

Silt (dark brown layer)

Fine sand

Coarse sand

In this example, the soil contained lots of sand and silt, but not much clay.

ROCK AGE AND STRATA

Rocks are always underfoot, but how do we know which rocks formed long ago and which ones formed more recently? For scientists who study fossils and ancient life (like the dinosaurs!), determining the age of rocks is essential, so how do they do it?

Try this: get some books and start stacking them up. Once you have a stack, take a look at it and its layers. Which layer is the oldest? It's the one at the bottom, the first book you set down. With sedimentary rocks, it's the same way! Sedimentary rocks form on the Earth's surface, and newer layers form on top of the older layers. A layer of rock is called a **stratum**, and many layers together are called **strata**. By looking at rock strata, we can figure out which layers are older than others, which helps us figure out how old the fossils in each layer may be.

While many sedimentary rocks are younger than other kinds of rocks, it's more difficult to figure out the age of igneous and

This illustration shows lots of rock strata. Soil is at the very top and the youngest layer of rock is just below it, and the oldest rock layer is at the bottom. Inside some of the layers are fossils, including a *Tyrannosaurus Rex* skull and a *Triceratops* skull. Which fossil is older?

The Grand Canyon in Arizona shows many sedimentary rock layers, with the oldest ones at the bottom of the canyon and the youngest at the top.

metamorphic rocks. That's because they don't often form in neat layers like sedimentary rocks. But by looking at certain minerals in the rocks, scientists in a lab can figure out how old they are. Some minerals—especially one called zircon—have elements in them that can slowly change over time. By carefully looking inside these minerals, scientists can figure out how much time has passed since they formed! Finding igneous or metamorphic rocks with zircons in them can therefore be very important for figuring out how old the Earth and its rocks are!

These dark-brown shapes are zircon crystals. Zircon can form as part of an igneous or metamorphic rock, and scientists can use them to figure out how long ago the rock formed.

Lumpy Strata

When you see cliffs or other rock formations that show lots of layers, you're seeing the strata (layers) of rock that formed over time. With sedimentary rock strata, each layer is older than the one above it. But even though many rock formations show strata that are very flat and even, not all of them formed that way! All kinds of things can happen that may make a layer lumpy or crooked. When the next layer forms on top of a lumpy layer, it will have a lump too, but not one as big. And as more layers build up, eventually they will smooth out again and be flat. You can see how this happens at home.

Start by getting 5 or 6 towels. You can get more than 6 if you want, but you should have at least 5. Next, put one towel down on a table and give it a big wrinkle or lump. This represents the first layer of sedimentary rock in your strata.

Then lay the other towels flat on top of the lumpy one. Place them neatly so that all their edges are lined up. Now what do you notice? The second towel you put down curves over the lumpy one, but the towel at the very top is a lot smoother, right? But it still isn't perfectly flat.

Now you can simulate millions of years of pressure inside the Earth by pressing down on the stack of towels. Watch what happens as you press harder and harder.

Not only did the stack of towels get flatter, but the curve caused by the bottom lumpy layer has now been smoothed out. The lump is still there in the bottom layer, but all the layers have now been compressed so hard that they fit more tightly together and make for a smoother, flatter rock formation.

We can see the same thing happen in real rocks. Next time you see a layered cliff, look for layers that aren't as flat and neat as the others. Once you spot one, look at how the lumpy or curved layer affected the layers above it. Here is a good example, shown below. How do you think compression affected this rock formation?

These upper layers are mostly flat and their shape isn't affected much by the lumpy layer below.

This thick layer filled in around the lumpy layer. It has a flatter top.

This older, deeper layer has a big lump in it that changed the shape of the next layer above it.

Fossils

Fossils are traces of plants and animals that have been left behind in sedimentary rocks. Normally, when a plant or animal dies, their bodies rot away and disappear. But if the plant or animal gets buried in mud and sediment, sometimes it won't rot away. Millions of years ago, when this happened to ancient plants and animals, their bodies became buried under many layers of sediment. Over time, as those layers compacted and hardened to become sedimentary rocks, the bodies of the plants and animals remained inside and became part of the rock.

When groundwater interacted with the dead plants and animals, it **deposited** (left behind) minerals in the tiny spaces inside their body parts. This happened most often with hard body parts, like bones, teeth, and shells. After a long time, the minerals from the ground completely filled the body part and **replaced** it, but still **preserved**, or kept, the shape of the body part. The result is a mineral formation with the same exact shape as the bone, tooth, shell, leaf, or branch that was once buried there!

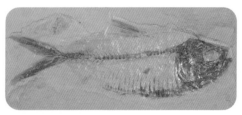

This is a fossil of an ancient fish skeleton in shale.

HOW BONES END UP INSIDE ROCKS

1. When this fish died, it sank to the bottom of a lake. Its soft parts, like skin and muscles, rotted away, leaving only the hard bones behind. Bones take a long time to break down.

2. Sediment sank down and buried the bones. Sometimes this happened slowly, but other times it happened fast in a landslide, when lots of dirt and mud moved all at once.

3. After the bones were completely buried, the weight of the sediment above began to compress them. The sediment was being compressed, too, and they began to stick together to form a rock with the bones trapped inside.

4. After a very long time, when the lake dried up and disappeared, the sediment was able to harden and turn into sedimentary rock. The hard rocks that held the bones inside also protected them, and the fish bones could stay preserved in the rock for millions of years!

There are other ways that fossils can form, but this is one of the common ways it happens.

Here are some common types of fossils found in sedimentary rocks all over the world:

Coral

Coral is a type of sea life that grows hard branching structures. Coral fossils are common, as coral have been living in Earth's oceans for millions of years (and still are today).

Snail Shells

Snails have no bones, but they do have a hard shell to protect them. Their shells grow little by little in a spiral shape. Snails have been living on Earth for a very long time, and their hard shells are often found as fossils inside rocks.

Bivalves and Brachiopods

These sea animals grow hard shells to protect themselves. The shells have two parts connected by a hinge so they can open.

Shark Teeth

Sharks are a special kind of fish that don't have hard bones. They have lived in Earth's oceans for millions of years, but we only have fossils of their teeth because they are the hardest parts of their bodies.

THE FOSSIL RECORD

To determine how old a fossil is, we can look at the rock strata around it, but we can also look at features of the fossil itself. Animals slowly change over time to better fit into their environment—this is called **evolution**. When we find a fossil, we can look at the layer of rock it was found within to give us an idea of how old it is. Then we can look at the features of the fossil and see how it compares to other similar fossils found in different layers of rock. We can use these comparisons to see how the animal changed over time. This is called the **fossil record**, and it is important for understanding life on Earth.

These spiral shells are fossil ammonites. Ammonites were like squids that had a hard spiral shell. They lived in the oceans for millions of years, and their shells grew in segments. As they evolved, the segments of their shells became more complex in shape. The ammonite shell on the bottom is an older one, found in lower layers of sedimentary rock. See how smooth its shell segments are? The ammonite on top is younger and was found in upper rock layers. See how squiggly and complicated its segments are?

HOW OLD IS THE EARTH?

Based upon everything scientists have learned so far, we know the Earth is just over **4.5 billion years old**—that's 4,500,000,000 years! When the Earth first formed, it was hot and probably had lots of melted rocks on the surface. But eventually, hundreds of millions of years later, it cooled down, and the surface of the Earth became the hard, rigid crust like we have today. Over billions of years, the tectonic plates moved around the planet and made many continents appear and disappear.

LIFE ON EARTH

We know from the fossil record that the first kinds of life were things like algae and bacteria (think of things like green pond scum), and they only lived in the oceans. It wasn't until just 541 million years ago that life began to be found all over, and it was only 419 million years ago that the first animals appeared on dry land! Dinosaurs first appeared around 233 million years ago (that's 233,000,000 years ago) and they may seem ancient, but sea animals like fish are much older! But almost all kinds of animals are older than humans—we've only been around for about 300,000 years! The chart on the next page shows the timeline of Earth and when certain plants and animals first appeared. At the very bottom is when Earth formed, around 4.5 billion years ago, and at the very top is today.

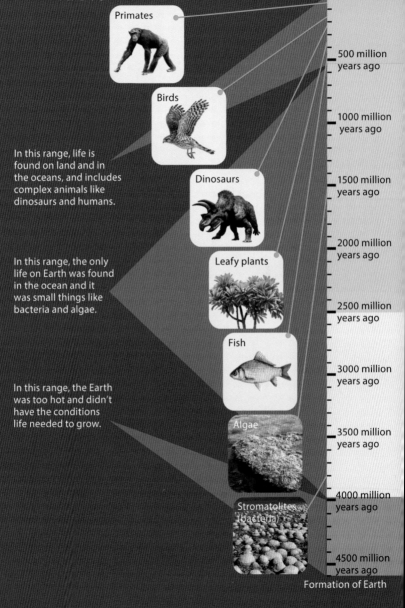

Today

Humans

Primates

500 million years ago

Birds

1000 million years ago

In this range, life is found on land and in the oceans, and includes complex animals like dinosaurs and humans.

Dinosaurs

1500 million years ago

2000 million years ago

Leafy plants

In this range, the only life on Earth was found in the ocean and it was small things like bacteria and algae.

2500 million years ago

Fish

3000 million years ago

In this range, the Earth was too hot and didn't have the conditions life needed to grow.

Algae

3500 million years ago

4000 million years ago

Stromatolites (bacteria)

4500 million years ago

Formation of Earth

Landforms

When you see an amazing mountain or beautifully layered cliff, you know that it's made of rock. But how did the mountains get so high? And what makes a cliff appear? All of the interesting shapes and features that you see in rocks around the world are caused by things like tectonic plate movements, rising magma, or by weathering and erosion. These cool places are called landforms, and from lakes to valleys to islands, landforms are what make our planet so fun to explore and learn about. In this chapter, we'll take a look at many of the land-forms you'll see around the world and how they came to be.

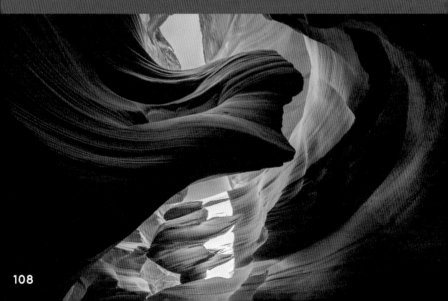

Mountains, Lakes, and More

Mountains, lakes, cliffs, and all of the other cool rock formations you may see when you're out in nature are examples of landforms. A **landform** is any feature of the Earth's surface that is distinct from other nearby features. For example, hills and mountains are landforms that are taller than the area surrounding them, and they are very different from a basin, which is a landform that is lower than the area surrounding it.

The low, flat area is a desert basin, and it is often hot and dry. It is a very different kind of landform than the tall mountains in the distance.

Landforms can form in a wide variety of ways, and lots of natural forces can help create them. Tectonic plate movements help make the biggest landforms, such as mountain ranges and oceans, and all of the heat and pressure that tectonic plates create can also cause other landforms to form. Magma deep below the surface can also help new landforms appear. If you need to review how tectonic plates move, go back to page 44.

The amazing landforms at Antelope Canyon, in Arizona, were formed by water wearing down sedimentary rocks and carrying away the little pieces that wore off them.

But tectonic plates and magma aren't the only ways landforms appear; weathering and erosion create lots of landforms, too. Weathering and erosion are when rocks are worn away and change shape and size because of water, wind, ice, and chemicals that

This lake formed in a low basin and is surrounded by high mountains. In the distance, you can see a small shoreline. These are all different kinds of landforms that formed in different ways.

chip away at them. Water and ice are two of the main forces that can change the shape of old rocks and cause them to turn into new landforms.

Water in rivers and oceans can also flow fast enough to carry and move sediments like sand and gravel. When the water slows down, the sediments sink and they, too, can cause new landforms to form.

In this book, we'll focus on landforms that form primarily from tectonic plate movements as well as those that form from weathering and erosion.

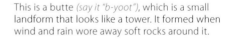

This is a butte *(say it "b-yoot")*, which is a small landform that looks like a tower. It formed when wind and rain wore away soft rocks around it.

OCEANS AND SEAS

Oceans are huge bodies of salty water, and a **sea** is similar but smaller. Most of the world's water is in the oceans, and the oceans are enormous—the Pacific Ocean alone is over 12,000 miles across!

When tectonic plates spread apart from each other (called **divergent movement**), it makes the continental crust thinner. At the thinnest part, the crust begins to crumble and collapse; this part is called a **rift**, and rifts are like big valleys. The thin crust in a rift allows the hot, soft rock from the asthenosphere to rise up because there is less weight pushing down on it. As the hot rock rises into the lithosphere and crust, it shoves the tectonic plates further away from each other. And when the soft, melted rock reaches the surface of the Earth, it cools to become new igneous rocks at the bottom of the rift.

As more hot rock rises, the rift is pushed wider and begins to collect water. When it's wide enough, we call it a sea, and eventually it can get so big that it becomes an ocean. This process is called **sea-floor spreading** because it happens on the floor of seas and oceans. Sea-floor spreading creates the thin, dark rock layers of oceanic crust.

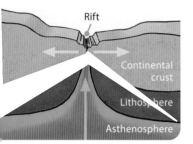

Rift

Continental crust

Lithosphere

Asthenosphere

When tectonic plates start to spread apart, it makes the continental crust above them thinner. Thin crust allows hot rock from the asthenosphere to rise up. This hot rock pushes the lithosphere and crust away from the center, making the crust even thinner and causing rocks to collapse into a big crack called a **rift**, or rift valley.

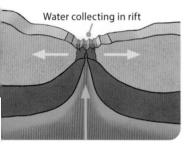

Water collecting in rift

When the hot, soft rock from the asthenosphere breaks the surface of the rift, it begins to cool and make new igneous rocks. As more soft melted rock rises, it pushes the new igneous rocks aside, too. The rift gets wider and deeper, and water collects.

The new igneous rocks become oceanic crust, and more water begins to collect to form a sea or ocean. Sea-floor spreading begins at the center of the rift where molten rock meets the surface. Because the rising rock pushes upward, this area is higher than the rest of the rift, and is called a **mid-ocean ridge**.

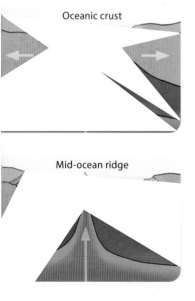

Oceanic crust

Mid-ocean ridge

There are many places around the Earth where we can see sea-floor spreading happening, or where we can find rifts that are just beginning to spread apart. The country of Iceland, in the northern Atlantic Ocean, is an island that formed on top of a mid-ocean ridge, which means that the oceanic crust is spreading apart right beneath Iceland! As a result, there are areas of Iceland where big long narrow valleys can be found, sometimes filled with water—these are the rift valleys. In the photo below, each side of the rift is on a different tectonic plate!

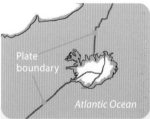

Iceland sits right on top of where two tectonic plates meet, called a plate boundary, shown by the red line. The plates are spreading apart, creating a rift, which you can see as a big valley. As the rift spreads apart, Iceland gets bigger!

The long and narrow Red Sea is a body of water in Northern Africa between the countries Egypt and Saudi Arabia. The Red Sea is actually a rift valley filled with water. It is much wider than the one in Iceland, and it gets a little wider every year because hot, soft rock is still rising and spreading Egypt and Saudi Arabia farther apart. Eventually, it could become big enough to be an ocean.

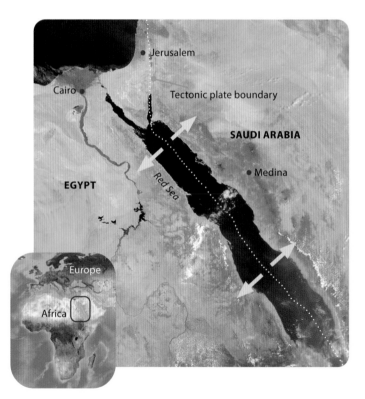

MOUNTAINS: PLATE COLLISIONS

A **mountain** is a high spot of land that rises at least 1,000 feet above the surrounding area. If you've ever been to a mountain, then you know how impressive they are! But how did they form? Well, there are a few different ways, but we'll start with mountains that form by tectonic plate collisions.

When two tectonic plates are moving toward each other (called convergent movement), they can press into each other so hard that one of them is forced up onto the other. This is called a **tectonic plate collision**, and they can be very powerful. They can cause lots of rock to crumple up and be squeezed upward, which becomes a mountain when it's been pushed high enough. When rocks rise upward, it is called **uplift**, and mountains are some of the biggest and most impressive examples of uplifted rocks.

Mountains don't usually form by themselves. They typically form in groups of mountains and hills along a line. A line of connected mountains and hills is called a **mountain range**, and some ranges can be thousands of miles long. The rocks inside a mountain range are often squeezed by so much pressure that some metamorphose, or change into metamorphic rocks. But not all of them do, especially those on the outer parts of a mountain range. This means that many mountain ranges are made of mixtures of lots of different kinds of rocks.

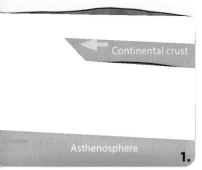

Two tectonic plates begin to collide and press into each other.

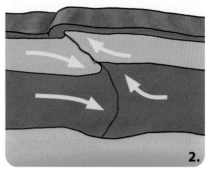

One plate begins to push itself on top of the other, which forces the other downward.

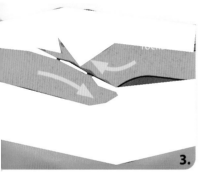

As the pressure builds, hills begin to form.

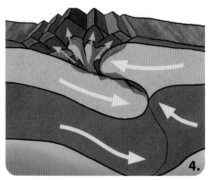

Eventually, rocks from the crust are forced upward in chunks that become mountains.

When two tectonic plates meet and push into each other, they begin to build a lot of pressure between them. Eventually, this causes one of the plates to start pushing upward on top of the other, which is forced downward.

As the two plates keep pressing together, the rocks that get squished between them can be changed and turned into metamorphic rocks (shown in these diagrams as the layered gray rocks). Chunks of the crust are pushed upward more and more and mountains start to form. As they get higher, big heavy pieces begin to break off and slide down, which gives the new mountains a sharp, jagged shape.

The Himalayas are the highest mountain range in the world. These jagged mountains formed when the tectonic plate beneath India collided with Asia. The plate collision uplifted enormous amounts of rock along the plate boundary. Even though the Himalayan Mountains are some of the highest mountains in the world, parts of them are made of sedimentary rocks that formed long ago at the bottom of an ocean! The uplift from the tectonic plate collision was so powerful that rocks that were once the sea floor have been pushed up high enough to become mountains! There are even ocean fossils at the top of Mt. Everest, the highest mountain in the world!

90 Million Years Ago

Today

MOUNTAINS: RIFTING, EXTENSION, AND FAULTING

Not all mountains form when tectonic plates collide—
some actually form when tectonic plates spread apart!
When tectonic plates below a continent begin to move
away from each other, it can stretch the crust thin,
just like pulling apart some stretchy pizza dough. This
is called **extension**, and it spreads out the crust and
makes it so thin and light that the hot, soft rising rocks
of the asthenosphere are able to push upward. The
rising asthenosphere uplifts the thin crust, making a
bulge. As the bulge gets bigger, the crust rocks begin
to **fault**, or break into big chunks. Some of the chunks
then **subside**, or sink into the crust.

As the bulge cracks and spreads apart, a **rift** forms
but does not fill with water to become a sea like the
kind we discussed earlier. As the extension continues
and the rift gets wider, bigger faults form and break
off huge chunks of rock that slide downward. The
result is a complex group of mountain ranges with lots
of alternating high and low areas.

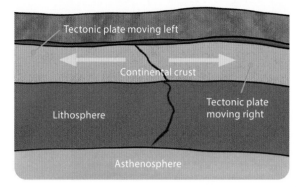

1. These two tectonic plates are beginning to separate and move away from each other.

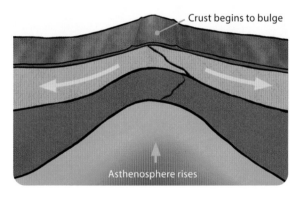

2. As the plates move apart, the continental crust is stretched thinner, which allows the hot, soft rock from the asthenosphere to rise and make the crust bulge upward.

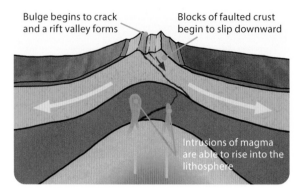

Bulge begins to crack and a rift valley forms

Blocks of faulted crust begin to slip downward

Intrusions of magma are able to rise into the lithosphere

3. As the bulge gets bigger, even more hot rock can rise, which makes the crust even thinner. The thin crust then starts to break and fault, collapsing in the middle to form a rift.

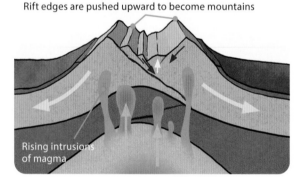

Rift edges are pushed upward to become mountains

Rising intrusions of magma

4. The rising magma pushes the bulge higher and the outer edges of the rift become tall mountains. Inside the rift, the crust forms huge faults that cause big blocks of rock to fall inward. Some may be squeezed upward, too.

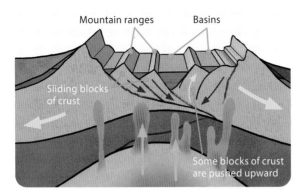

Mountain ranges   Basins

Sliding blocks of crust

Some blocks of crust are pushed upward

5. As the rift valley extends wider, the faulted blocks inside the rift can become their own mountains. The low areas between each row of mountains are called basins, which can fill with sediment to create low, flat areas.

If it looks like a complicated process, that's because it is! There are a lot of forces at work inside the Earth when these kinds of mountain ranges form. But there are many places around the world where we can see that it happened. In many western states, such as Nevada, Utah, California, and Arizona, we can find mountain ranges separated by low, flat areas formed by extension and faulting of the crust. This kind of landscape is called **basin-and-range**, because many mountain ranges are separated by many basins, or low areas.

The photo below was taken in a basin-and-range area in Death Valley, California. The person who took the photo was standing on one mountain range and was looking across a basin toward another mountain range. This formed when continental crust extended.

MOUNTAINS: VOLCANIC ARCS AND HOT SPOT VOLCANOES

Mountains can form in and around oceans too. When a tectonic plate under an ocean collides with a tectonic plate under a continent, the thin, heavy oceanic plate is forced underneath the thick continental plate. This is called **subduction** *(say it "sub-duck-shun")*, and the oceanic plate will be forced down into the asthenosphere where it melts! Most oceanic plates are subducted below continental plates near the coastlines of the continents.

When an oceanic plate melts beneath the edge of a continental plate, it turns into lots of hot, soft magma. That magma rises and is forced upward through the continental plate until it breaks the surface of the continental crust. This can uplift lots of rocks, and when the magma reaches the surface and cools, it forms lots of new rocks, too. After enough time, a mountain range forms near the ocean coast. Many of the mountains here can be volcanoes as well. This type of mountain range is called a **volcanic arc**, because the line of mountains often forms in a big curving arc shape near a continent's coast.

A **hot spot volcano** is a volcanic mountain that rises from the ocean floor to form an island. Rising hot rock from the asthenosphere is able to force itself through the thin oceanic crust. When the hot rock hits the cold ocean water, it cools and forms igneous rocks. When this happens over a long time, enough new igneous rocks build up to make an island. But the volcano keeps erupting and adding new rocks to the island, making it bigger every year. Iceland and Hawaii are two examples of hot spot volcano islands. They are called "hot spots" because they form at a spot in the oceanic crust that is much hotter than the crust around it. But because the oceanic crust moves along with the tectonic plates below it, the hot spots move, too. That means that a hot spot doesn't just make one island, it can form many islands in a row!

VOLCANIC ARCS

There are several volcanic arc mountain ranges around the world, but the Pacific Northwest of the United States and Canada is a very good example of one. Off the coast of Washington, Oregon, and

California, a tectonic plate called the Juan de Fuca plate is subducting, or sinking, beneath the much larger North American tectonic plate. The Juan de Fuca plate is a heavy, thin oceanic plate, so it is being forced beneath the thick continental North American plate. As the Juan de Fuca plate gets pushed deeper and deeper, it sinks down into the asthenosphere, where it melts. The hot melted rock is then squeezed upward by the pressure of the two tectonic plates pushing together. When the melted rock reaches the surface of the Earth, it forms a range of volcanoes and mountains. In the Pacific Northwest, the subduction of the Juan de Fuca plate formed the Cascade Range of mountains, which contains many active volcanoes!

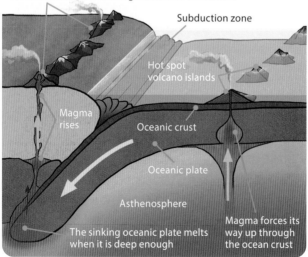

A volcano forms where magma reaches the surface

Subduction zone

Hot spot
volcano islands

Magma
rises

Oceanic crust

Oceanic plate

Asthenosphere

The sinking oceanic plate melts
when it is deep enough

Magma forces its
way up through
the ocean crust

Mt. Shasta is a volcano in the Cascade Range

The Cascade Range Volcanic Arc

NORTH AMERICAN TECTONIC PLATE

Mt. Baker

WASHINGTON
Mt. Rainier

Mt. St. Helens

JUAN DE FUCA TECTONIC PLATE (moving eastward)

Subduction zone

Mt. Hood

OREGON

Crater Lake

Pacific Ocean

Mt. Shasta

CALIFORNIA

This map shows the Cascade Range volcanoes (the volcanoes are the red triangles). The mountain range, shaded in yellow, has an arc shape. The red line is where the Juan de Fuca plate is disappearing beneath the North American plate, which is called a **subduction zone**, because that's where subduction is happening.

HOT SPOT VOLCANOES

The Hawaiian islands are one of the best examples of hot spot volcanoes. Located in the middle of the Pacific Ocean, the Hawaiian islands formed when magma forced its way up through the thin oceanic crust. When the hot rock touched the cold seawater, it hardened to form igneous rocks. Over a long time, so much rock built up that it formed an underwater mountain, and the tip of the mountain eventually rose above the waves to become an island.

But because the tectonic plate below a hot spot volcano is slowly moving, it can form one volcano in one place, then a new volcano in another place later on. In fact, one hot spot can make a whole string of volcanic islands! This is called an **island chain**, and they can show us where the tectonic plate has moved.

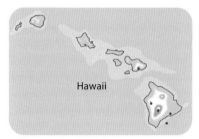

Hawaii

This is a map of the Hawaiian Island chain in the Pacific Ocean. The red dots are active volcanoes.

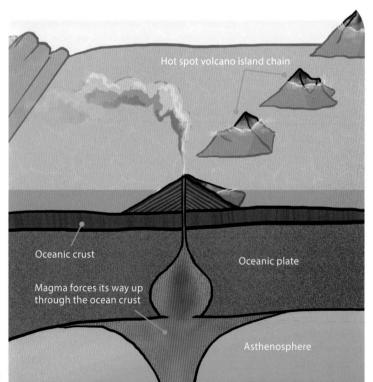

Hot spot volcano island chain

Oceanic crust

Oceanic plate

Magma forces its way up through the ocean crust

Asthenosphere

This is one of the Hawaiian Islands. This photo was taken from space. The white circle near the middle is the snowy top of a tall volcano.

Two of the Hawaiian Islands are still growing bigger as more volcanic eruptions keep happening and adding more rock to the islands.

Some eruptions take place right by the ocean. Hot lava pours into the water and cools very fast, making huge amounts of steam!

ROCK-FORMING ENVIRONMENTS: A SUMMARY

In this book, you've learned a lot about the Earth and its igneous, sedimentary, and metamorphic rocks. But let's review where some of those rocks are formed:

1. Rising magma cools to form intrusive igneous rock (plutons).

2. The heat from rising magma can change the older rocks around it to turn them into metamorphic rocks (called contact metamorphism).

3. Tectonic plate collisions make high pressure that turns older rocks into metamorphic rocks.

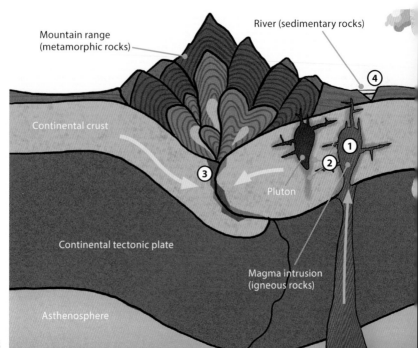

Mountain range (metamorphic rocks)

River (sedimentary rocks)

Continental crust

Pluton

Continental tectonic plate

Magma intrusion (igneous rocks)

Asthenosphere

4. Sediments sink to the bottom of rivers and lakes and compress to form sedimentary rocks.

5. Magma gets forced to the surface where a volcano forms and produces extrusive igneous rocks.

6. Sediments at the bottom of the ocean form sedimentary rocks.

7. Sea-floor spreading forms new igneous rocks.

8. Subduction (sinking) of oceanic plates causes the rock to melt and become magma, which rises and cools to form igneous rocks.

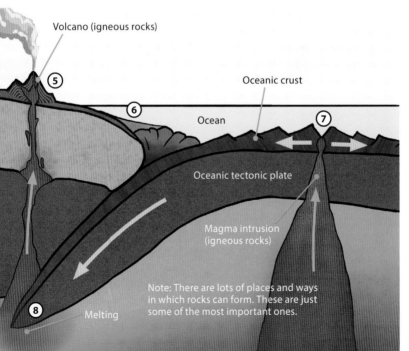

Volcano (igneous rocks)

⑤

Oceanic crust

⑥

Ocean

⑦

Oceanic tectonic plate

Magma intrusion
(igneous rocks)

⑧

Melting

Note: There are lots of places and ways in which rocks can form. These are just some of the most important ones.

Weathering and Erosion

Many other kinds of landforms form when old rocks are weathered and eroded. **Weathering** is what happens when things like ice and chemicals cause large bodies of rock to change shape and size. Weathering can make big cracks appear in rock or cause rocks to collapse entirely. Weathering wears away rocks without moving them, but **erosion** removes pieces from rocks and moves them to new places. Erosion happens when things like wind and flowing water cause little pieces of a rock to come off and wash or blow away as sediment. Both weathering and erosion happen very slowly, but they can cause even mountains to turn into grains of sand!

Erosion and weathering often cause older rocks and landforms to become smaller and smoother. You can easily see this when you compare the Rocky Mountains to the Appalachian Mountains. The Rocky Mountains are younger, so they are still high and jagged. The Appalachian Mountains are much older, and weathering has made them lower and smoother.

The Rocky Mountains are still jagged, pointy, and tall because they are younger.

The Appalachian Mountains are lower and more rounded because they are older.

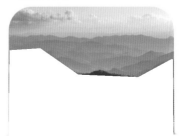

EROSION

Erosion *(say it "ee-ro-shun")* happens when wind, rain, waves, and glaciers (big sheets of moving ice) hit or scrape against rocks and remove little pieces from them to become sediments.

TYPES OF WEATHERING

Mechanical weathering happens when forces cause huge rock formations to break right where they stand, without moving. Heat from the sun, ice that forms in cracks in the rock, salt from the oceans, and even the roots of plants can cause a rock formation to break. Mechanical weathering happens best in cold, dry regions.

Chemical weathering happens when chemicals in water dissolve the minerals in rocks and wash them away. Acids are the most common reason for chemical weathering.
Acids are chemicals that can more easily cause materials to dissolve. Plants and animals can create acids that can make certain rocks dissolve and wash away. Chemical weathering often gives rocks round pits, and it can even make huge rock formations collapse! Chemical weathering happens best in hot, wet regions.

EROSION OF THE LANDSCAPE

Most erosion happens on the Earth's surface because that's where things like rain and rivers can move and break down rocks. And when a lot of water wears away rocks for a very long time, it creates tons of grains of sediment (like sand) that wash down rivers and settle into the oceans. But even though it seems like erosion and weathering would only affect rocks on the surface, it can cause changes deep underground.

Softer rocks (like sedimentary rocks) erode and weather away much faster than harder rocks (like igneous rocks). Since most sedimentary rocks form on the Earth's surface and many igneous rocks form deep down below them, erosion and weathering can cause the softer sedimentary rocks to wear away completely to reveal the igneous rocks. This means that rocks that formed very deep in the Earth can be found on the surface where we can see them!

When rocks on the Earth's surface erode and break down into sediments that wash into the oceans, that removes a lot of weight from the continent. After a very long time, tons and tons of rock can be worn away, which means there is a lot less weight pushing down on the rocks below the surface. That means that the hot asthenosphere is able to push upward more easily, causing rocks that were once deeply buried inside the Earth to rise up to where we can see them! This is a kind of uplift, and it is how many plutons (see page 59 to remember what those are) rise up to the Earth's surface.

The illustrations below show how erosion can wear away the top rock strata and expose lower rocks over millions of years. They also show how the asthenosphere can rise and push rocks upward when there's less weight pushing down on it.

5 million years ago

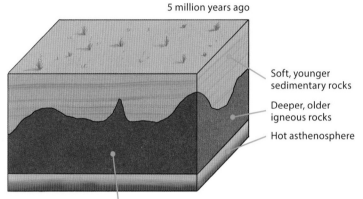

Soft, younger sedimentary rocks

Deeper, older igneous rocks

Hot asthenosphere

Igneous rock formations that become exposed at the surface after the sedimentary rocks erode away

Today

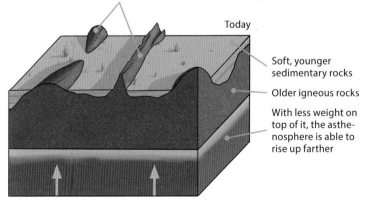

Soft, younger sedimentary rocks

Older igneous rocks

With less weight on top of it, the asthenosphere is able to rise up farther

WATER: RIVERS, WAVES, AND RAIN

As rain falls, water can loosen and remove tiny grains from rock. But it's a slow process. Water can erode rocks much more quickly on the coasts of lakes and oceans where waves crashing against rocks are much stronger. This can cause lots of material to wear off of the rocks. Rivers are also very good at eroding rocks, especially rivers that flow very quickly. As the flowing water washes over rocks, it can pull pieces off of them and push them down the river. Rivers are full of sediments like sand and rounded pebbles that were removed from larger bodies of rock that the river flowed over.

Waves and rivers can wash away so much rock that they can change the shape of huge rock formations like cliffs and islands. Fast moving rivers can also wash away so much rock that they become deeper and wider as time goes on.

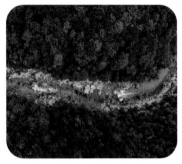

This photo was taken from the air and shows a fast-moving river carving its way through a forest.

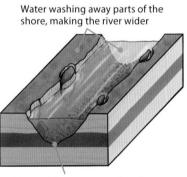

Water washing away parts of the shore, making the river wider

Water pushing away gravel and sand, making the river deeper

RIVERS, SEDIMENTS, AND STREAM LOAD

Rivers and streams can move rocks and sediments. But faster rivers can move way more rocks and sediments than slow rivers. Faster rivers can also move bigger rocks and sediments than slow rivers can.

Since it's easier for the water in a river to move lightweight sediments like silt and clay, even slow-moving rivers can carry those sediments a long distance. But only fast-moving rivers can carry heavy sediments like sand and gravel. And when a fast-moving river carrying gravel, sand, silt, and clay slows down, the gravel sinks and stops moving first because it is heaviest. As the river gets slower, then the sand sinks and settles, and then the silt and clay can only settle when the water is very slow or even completely still. The ability for rivers and streams of different speeds to carry different-sized sediment is called **stream load**.

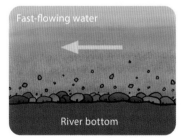

A fast-moving river has a lot of energy, so it can move lots of tiny sediments, like sand and silt, as well as bigger ones like gravel. See how the water looks dirty?

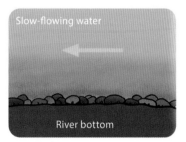

A slow-moving river has less energy, so it can only move some tiny sediments like clay. See how this water is clearer and has fewer sediments carried in it?

ROUNDING SEDIMENTS

As rocks and pebbles are rolled down a river or along a beach by the water, they bump into each other a lot. As they do, they chip and break each other's hard edges and sharp corners. Eventually, after a very long time rolling along the bottom of rivers, the rocks become smaller and rounder. You've probably seen rivers or beaches full of round stones that were shaped when they were rolled around in gravel and sand for millions of years.

Sediments and rocks also can become very round in dry places, too, because windblown sand can erode and shape rocks even better than water can.

This blocky piece of wax was worn down into a more round shape by rolling on the ground.

Mini-Activity: Shaping Sediments

You can see how sediment becomes rounded by taking a piece of hard wax or clay and cutting it into a square shape, or breaking it into a shape with lots of sharp edges and angles. Then, take it for a walk! Go outside and kick it around, rolling it around the sidewalk and bouncing it along the ground. After a while, take a look at it. You'll see that lots of the sharp edges and corners have been chipped off.

WIND AND ICE

Wind can blow away tiny loose pieces from rocks, especially in dry areas without many plants, like deserts. And when wind is blowing little grains of sediment, like sand, the grains can hit other rocks and break off other tiny pieces from them, too. Wind-blown sand, for example, can be very damaging to other rocks, some-times even wearing holes right through whole cliffs!

When the wind blows sand, it can be very damaging to rocks. This rock arch was made by wind-blown sand hitting it for thousands of years.

In cold climates, ice can weather and break rocks, too. Water expands (gets bigger) when it freezes into ice, so when some water gets into a crack in a rock and freezes, the ice can actually push the crack bigger. After enough cold winters, the repeated freezing of

ice in a crack can actually split the rock open!

After many winters, freezing temperatures caused water inside the cracks in this rock to freeze and expand, which made the cracks bigger and broke up the rock.

PLANTS AND SALT

You may think of rocks as being much tougher than plants, but plants can actually break rocks! When a plant grows above rocks, its roots can grow into cracks in

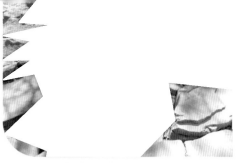

The roots of this old tree have grown into spaces in the rock and cracked it as the roots grew larger.

the rock when they're still little. As the plant grows bigger, their roots do, too, and the widening roots can split the rock apart! This can happen on the edges of cliffs and cause them to collapse.

On the coasts of oceans, rocks on the shore get lots of seawater splashed on them. The seawater in oceans is very salty because it has lots of salt and other minerals dissolved in it. When it splashes into

This strange seaside rock was weathered by sea salt.

cracks and little spaces in rocks, salt crystals can pre-cipitate out of the water when it dries up. As the salt crystals grow bigger, they can push little grains off of the rock and start to make a hole. After a long time, salt crystals can make lots of strange holes in seaside rocks! This is called **salt weathering**.

GROUNDWATER AND ACIDS

Not all water is on the Earth's surface where we can see it—there's a lot of water underground, too. We call it **groundwater**, and it can be found inside the little spaces within rocks and soil beneath our feet. Wells get their water from groundwater.

But groundwater can also affect the rocks that hold it, especially if the water has some natural acids in it. This can dissolve some kinds of rock, creating caves and other spaces in the Earth. Rocks dissolving in groundwater can also create sinkholes, which are where the surface rocks collapse downward into a hole in the ground (we'll talk more about sinkholes later). Other times, underwater rivers can cause valleys and other landforms to form on the surface above them.

This underground river has made a path for itself by dissolving and eroding the soft rock.

Groundwater can create spaces underground that make the surface weak. Sometimes these weak spots can collapse and form a sinkhole.

GLACIERS

Glaciers are one of the most powerful sources of erosion. A **glacier** is an enormous sheet of ice that forms when tons of snow builds up and compresses (squashes together) over a long period of time. As more ice grows on the glacier, it gets so heavy that it begins to flow very slowly downhill, sometimes moving only a few inches a day. Today, most glaciers are only found high on cold mountains. But long ago, during the **Ice Ages** (when the temperature around the world was cooler), glaciers formed across the land and slowly moved from the cold north and south poles into warmer areas. Many of those huge glaciers were thousands of feet thick and many miles wide!

When glaciers get too warm, they begin to melt and get smaller. This makes them flow in the other direction. Today, glaciers are becoming rarer because the Earth is getting too warm for many of them. Pollution made by humans is causing glaciers to melt faster than we've ever seen before.

This mountain glacier is in Iceland. It is flowing slowly down the mountain. Every time it snows, the glacier gets a little thicker and can flow farther. The ice in a glacier can look blue because it is packed so tightly together. The cracks in the ice are caused by the sun and by the movement of the ice.

This huge mountain glacier in Canada has carved a wide valley into the rock. Look at how much more snow is at the top of the mountain; that is where the glacier first formed before it started flowing down the mountain.

Glacier
This enormous mass of ice slowly grows and moves downhill.

Gravel and Sand
When the ice melts, the gravel and sand inside of it are left behind as hills and ridges.

Rivers and Lakes
The melting ice in a glacier leaves behind lots of water, which forms into lakes and rivers that flow away from the glacier.

Crushed Rock
Glaciers crush rock into little pieces of sand and gravel that get stuck in the ice. Glaciers are very dirty!

Glaciers are extremely heavy, and the ice can crush the rocks beneath it! As glaciers move, they scrape and break up the rocks below, and when a pebble is loosened from the Earth, the freezing ice can lift it off the ground. The pebble then gets frozen into the ice. This is called **plucking**, and when a glacier has plucked lots of rock, it makes the ice dirty and more rough, so it scrapes the land even more. Because the heavy, rough ice of a glacier gets so full of rocks, they can carve wide valleys in between mountains and scrape the land smooth. At the front of a glacier, a lake and rivers often form. And when a glacier melts, it leaves all of the rocks in it behind as piles and ridges of gravel and sand.

Glacial Plucking

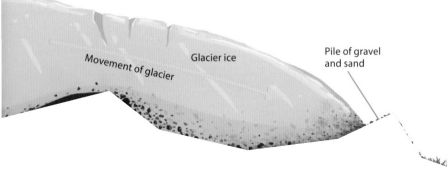

Movement of glacier

Glacier ice

Pile of gravel and sand

As the weight of the glacier crushes the rock below it, small pieces come off as gravel and sand. The freezing ice then sticks to the broken rocks and plucks it off the ground and into the ice. All of the rocks stuck in the ice make the glacier scrape and carve the land more.

This mountain glacier in Switzerland has scraped away so much rock that it has carved its own valley! The ice looks gray because it has so much gravel and sand in it, which was made when the ice crushed the mountain rock. The lake at the bottom of the glacier is forming as the ice melts.

These strange, smooth grooves in the hard rock were made when a glacier flowed over it. The rough rocks and gravel frozen inside the glacier's ice acted like sandpaper and scraped and carved the rock. The glacier melted away a long time ago, but we know it was here because of this rock's smooth, carved surfaces.

LANDSLIDES

A **landslide** is a type of erosion where lots of rock and soil moves downhill all at once. Landslides can be big or small, but they are often very destructive. They can be caused by many different things, too. Many landslides happen when lots of rain or groundwater soaks the side of a mountain or hill, and the wet ground begins to slide down. Other times, earthquakes or volcanic eruptions can shake the ground so much that rocks begin to slide down the side of a mountain or hill. Landslides can even happen underwater, especially in the oceans near the shore.

Plants and water caused this small landslide to drop boulders and dirt on this road.

Lots of rainfall caused this huge landslide to fall down the side of this mountain, making lots of mud and burying a farm.

METEORITE IMPACTS

A rare type of erosion is a meteorite impact. A **meteorite** *(say it "me-tee-or-ite")* is a rock from space, sometimes made of metal, that falls to Earth. When it impacts, or hits the ground, it can make a round bowl-shaped hole called a **crater**, which has high walls. A crater can form in any kind of rock because the meteorite lands with so much speed that it can punch into anything it hits. A meteorite impact can also be so powerful that it can throw pieces of rock miles away!

You might have seen a bright, fiery shooting star in the night sky before—that's a meteor falling from space! Once it hits the ground, then we call it a meteorite. But most never hit the ground because they are too small and burn up before they land.

This is an artist's picture of what a huge meteor might look like before it hits the Earth.

This huge crater in Arizona was formed when a meteorite the size of four buses hit the Earth thousands of years ago.

Landforms Formed by Weathering and Erosion

Like tectonic plate movements, weathering and erosion are so powerful that they can carve and shape the land into amazing landforms. In this section, we'll talk about some important landforms made by weathering and erosion.

RIVERS AND RIVER VALLEYS

Water always flows downhill, so water that flows away from mountains and other high areas will collect to form streams and rivers. **Rivers** are channels of water that flow over the land. All rivers are very good at carrying away soil and rocks and washing them away to lakes and oceans far away. Over lots of time, a flowing river will erode and wash away so much of the rock beneath it that it becomes deeper and wider. And after a very long time, a river can cut down through rocks to form a river valley or a canyon.

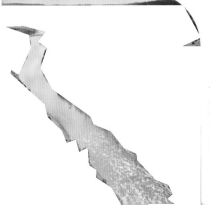

This fast-moving river has cut deeply into the surrounding hills. The river used to flow over the top of these hills, but as the river washed away more and more rock, it got lower and lower and now cuts through the hills. This is a **river valley**.

A **canyon** is formed when a river erodes through rock for a very long time. Canyons are river valleys that are very deep and have steep sides. The Grand Canyon in Arizona is one of the most famous examples.

Many river valleys are narrow and steep, but some like this one become much wider and flatter. This is because rivers can change their path over time, or become wider or thinner or faster or slower, due to how much water is washing into them.

A **waterfall** is where a river drops off the edge of a cliff or other steep landform. The falling water erodes the rock below it very quickly and can form a deep pool at the bottom.

CLIFFS, MESAS, AND BUTTES

Water can erode and wash away little pieces and grains from any kind of rock, if given enough time. Softer rocks, such as sedimentary rocks, erode more quickly, and harder rocks, such as igneous and metamorphic rocks, erode slower. But all rocks will eventually become weaker and erode in water.

Cliffs are one of the landforms that result when water and other forces weaken rocks and wash away parts of them. A **cliff** is a vertical (straight up and down) edge of a rock formation that formed when erosion caused rocks to collapse and fall. This can happen anywhere, but it is very common on the coasts of oceans. The waves crash against the rocks and wash away little pieces of them day after day. Eventually, the rocks become weak and fall down under their own weight. When the rocks fall, a new cliff is formed,

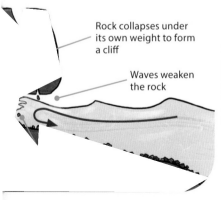

Rock collapses under its own weight to form a cliff

Waves weaken the rock

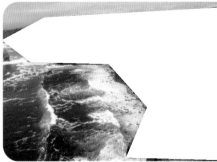

Cliffs form when waves wash away lower parts of the rock, which causes the upper part to fall down under its own weight.

which will also start to erode. Plant roots on top of the cliffs will erode them, too, causing them to collapse from above.

Mesas *(say it "may-sas")* are high areas that have a flat top and are surrounded on all sides by cliffs. There are usually steep piles of loose rock at the bottom of

the cliffs. Mesas form when rain and other weathering washes away softer rocks, leaving harder rocks behind. The harder rocks become the tops of the mesas, almost like a hard cap that protects the rock below it. Mesas are common in desert areas.

Buttes *(say it "b-yoots")* are a lot like mesas but are smaller and usually more steep. They have a flat top and cliffs on all sides. They also form when rain and other weather washes away softer rocks, leaving the harder rocks behind, and they can look like natural rock towers.

LAKES AND PONDS

Lakes and **ponds** are bodies of water formed when water collects in a low spot. Water always flows downhill, so it will always collect in the lowest spot around. Weathering and erosion, especially glaciers, will wear away soil and rocks and make a **basin**, which is a low, bowl-shaped area where water can collect. Small basins make ponds and large ones make lakes. Ponds and lakes can be found along rivers and often have rivers connecting to them.

Lakes are most common in the northern parts of the world because one of the main ways they formed was by glaciers. As the glaciers disappeared, they left behind huge chunks of ice that melted slowly. The melting ice chunks, combined with all of the gravel and sand that came out of the melting glaciers, formed basins. And with lots of melting ice comes a lot of water, so the water collected in the basins came from the melting ice. That is one of the reasons northern places like Canada and Russia have so many lakes.

MORAINES AND DRUMLINS

Glaciers are huge, heavy sheets of ice that can move lots of rocks and gravel around. They are so powerful that they can create their own landforms! The ice in a glacier is very dirty and full of gravel and sand. When a glacier melts, it leaves it all behind as a ridge or hill called a **moraine**. And when a glacier moves over the landscape, piles of gravel build up in pockets underneath it. After the glacier melts, those rocky piles are left behind as hills called **drumlins**.

These hills are lined up in the same direction. That's because they actually formed beneath a glacier long ago. After the glacier melted, the hills remained. Hills that form beneath a glacier are called **drumlins**, and they are often long and all go in the same direction.

This glacier is flowing down from the mountains in the background. See how dirty the ice is? The ridge of gravel in front of the glacier, between it and the lake, is a **moraine**. The dirt and rocks in the ice is being left behind on the moraine.

LANDFORMS THAT CAN BE FORMED BY EROSION OR BY TECTONIC PLATE MOVEMENTS (OR BOTH!)

Many kinds of landforms can actually be formed by both tectonic plate movements and by erosion! Let's take a look at some important ones:

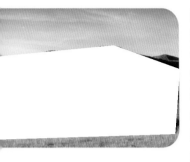

Hills are landforms that are higher than the area around them, but not as high as a mountain. Hills may seem like simple bumps in the land, but there are actually many kinds of hills! Many hills are formed when rain and rivers carve the landscape and wash away soil and rock from lower areas. But some hills are formed when tectonic plates collide, just like some mountains. In fact, many hills are found on either side of a mountain range—those are called foothills.

Plateaus *(say it "plat-ohs")* are flat areas that are higher than the land around them. They may resemble a mesa, but they are not surrounded on all sides by cliffs—usually they just have cliffs on one side. Plateaus can form when rivers and rain wash away rock on the lower side, but they can also form when tectonic movements or rising magma push rock formations upward.

An **escarpment** *(say it "ess-carp-ment")* is a long cliff that separates a higher area from a lower area. For example, the cliffs along the side of a plateau are an escarpment. And just like with plateaus, an escarpment can form when water erodes the lower side and also when tectonic movements and faults cause one side to rise or fall.

A **valley** is a long, low area between two high areas, especially mountains. Valleys often have a V-shape and usually have a river that runs along the bottom of them. Some valleys were formed when a river washed away lots of rock, but most valleys start forming when tectonic plates push

together to form hills and mountains that have lots of low areas between them. Those low areas begin to collect water, and rivers form and begin to flow downhill. Over time, the rivers make the low areas even lower, cutting v-shape valleys into the rock.

SHORELINES: BEACHES, BAYS, AND MORE

The shoreline along a big body of water, such as an ocean or lake, can have lots of different landforms. Many of them are formed when the wind and waves erode the rocks, but others are formed when tectonic plates cause rocks to raise or lower into the water. Some can even be formed by both at once.

Beaches are low, sloping areas where the water meets the shore. Most beaches are covered with rounded gravel or sand that the waves pushed there. Below the sand on most beaches is bedrock that slopes downward beneath the surface

of the ocean. In many cases, tectonic plate movements formed the shoreline, but erosion covered the beaches in sand and gravel.

A **bay** is a body of water that is open on one side and connects to a larger body of water. Many bays are shaped like a U and people use them to protect their boats from ocean waves. Bays can form when waves erode soft rocks, but they can also form from tectonic plate movements and rising magma that create new landforms on the coasts of continents.

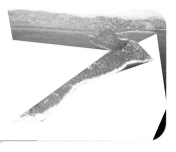

Peninsulas *(say it "pen-in-soo-las")* are strips of land that are surrounded by water on almost all sides. They are connected to the mainland on just one side, and peninsulas are often narrow and can be very long. They can form when erosion washes away the land around them, but they most often form when tectonic plate movements or volcanic eruptions create harder rock that becomes surrounded by water. Sometimes weathering can wear away a peninsula's connection to the mainland, leaving it surrounded on all sides by water and making it an island.

An **island** is a piece of land that is completely surrounded by water and is not connected to any larger piece of land. Islands can be big or tiny, and they can be made of different kinds of rock or sediments depending on where they are. Many

tropical islands are made of sedimentary rocks and sediments like coral and sand, but hot spot volcanic islands and many Arctic islands are made of volcanic rock that rose up into the ocean during tectonic plate movements and volcanic eruptions of lava. Sometimes the strong waves of the ocean can weather and erode peninsulas and other landforms to create islands, too.

The Water Cycle: How It Affects and Creates Landforms and Environments

The way water moves around the Earth in oceans, clouds, plants, and in the ground is called **the water cycle**. Every part of the water cycle is connected, and each part is important because they all can change rocks and landforms. But landforms can change where water is found and how it moves, too.

Water can change forms—it can be a liquid, it can be a solid (called ice), and it can be a gas (called steam). These changes happen because of how hot or cold its molecules are. When the sun's heat warms up water in a lake, pond, or ocean, it can cause some of the water to turn into gas and rise up into the air. That's called **evaporation**. Have you ever seen a puddle after a rainstorm dry up in the sunlight? The water didn't just disappear, it turned to gas and rose up into the sky!

When water is in the sky, it takes the form of clouds. Clouds are lightweight and can blow around and travel long distances in the air. Eventually, the water molecules in clouds can clump together and get so heavy that they fall—that's rain! And if it is cold enough to freeze water, it will instead fall from the clouds as snow.

Water is also found underground, and most places around the world hold lots of water deep down in rocks. The water there isn't like a lake or pond, though. Instead, it is soaked into all the tiny

little spaces and cracks in the rock. It's kind of like a sponge—when a sponge is full of water, you can't always see the water because it's trapped inside all the tiny spaces within the sponge. The water that's trapped underground is called the **water table**, and it is very important for people because lots of our drinking water comes from wells that are dug down into areas with lots of water, called **aquifers** *(say it "awk-wif-er")*.

Places that hold water—like lakes, oceans, clouds, glaciers, and the water table—are called **reservoirs** *(say it "rez-erv-wor")*. But there is one more kind of natural reservoir: plants! All the lush, green plants are holding water, too, and they can release it through evaporation. Reservoirs, rain, snow, and plants work together to make the water cycle.

THE WATER CYCLE

Here's a look at how all the different parts of the
water cycle work together to move water around.
The water cycle can weather and erode rocks, but
rock formations (such as mountains) can also affect
how the water cycle works!

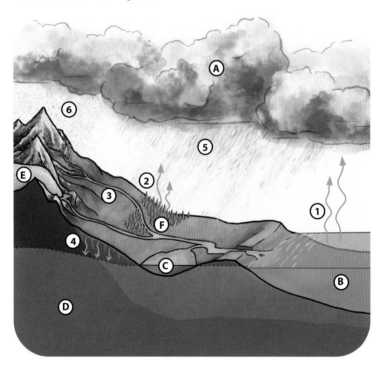

Remember that water can be found in three forms:
liquid water (like in a lake or river), gas (like in steam,
when water evaporates and dries up), and ice (solid,
frozen water, like in ice and snow).

RESERVOIRS

On the illustration, all of the things labeled with letters are reservoirs, where water is held. They are:

A. Clouds (liquid water droplets in the air)
B. Oceans (water in the form of liquid)
C. Lakes and rivers (water in the form of liquid)
D. Water table (water in the form of liquid trapped in rock) [shown as the blue-shaded area underground]
E. Glaciers and snow (water in the form of a solid)
F. Plants (water in the form of liquid trapped in plants)

HOW WATER MOVES

In the illustration, all of the things labeled with numbers are the different ways water is moved around. They are:

1. Evaporation from oceans, lakes, ponds, and rivers (water turning into a gas and rising into the air)
2. Evaporation from plants
3. Water flowing downhill, especially from melting mountain snow, ice, and glaciers
4. Water seeping down into the ground to join the water table
5. Rain falling from clouds
6. Snow falling from clouds in colder places and on mountains

After studying the water cycle, can you think of how water from snow melting on a mountain might get all the way to the ocean? Or how about a way that water would get from the ocean all the way up to a mountain top? And now can you see how water washing down from the mountains could carry sand and gravel all the way to the ocean?

Where Is the Water Table?

The water table is what we call all the water trapped underground inside rocks. But it can be hard to imagine what the water table looks like. It isn't like an underground lake or ocean; it's more like a kitchen sponge that is filled with water. In a full sponge, you can't really see the water, but it's there, trapped inside all the little holes and spaces in the sponge. In the water table, all the water is trapped inside the tiny spaces inside rocks. But we know it's there, because we can dig a hole down into the rocks and the water will leak out of the tiny spaces and begin to fill the hole we dug (that's called a well). Here's a simple activity you can do at home to see how the water table works. You'll need:

- A shallow pan
- Water
- Sand
- A spoon

Fill a shallow pan about halfway with water.

Then, carefully pour sand into the tray until you can no longer see the water. The water is still there, but it is underneath the surface of the sand (the sand will be wet, but that's OK). The sand represents rocks, and the water hidden inside of it represents the water table, trapped in all the tiny spaces between the grains of sand.

Next, with a spoon, start to dig a little hole in the middle of the sand.

Is the hole filling with water? That's because the water trapped in between the sand grains is able to leak into the hole you dug in the sand. If you keep digging wider and deeper, you'll find that the water keeps leaking out of the sand and into the hole. This is how the water table works! You can try this with different kinds of sand or dirt, and with more or less water. What happens when you scoop all the water out of the hole?

PLAINS

There are many ways that the water cycle can not only change rock formations, but can even create new landforms! One example of a landform that can be made by the water cycle is a plain. You've probably seen plains before—a **plain** is a large, mostly flat area that doesn't have a lot of trees. Plains can be many miles wide and often make good farmland. They can form a few different ways, but how does the water cycle create plains?

Fast-flowing water can pick up sediments, especially tiny sediments like clay. But slow-moving water can't move sediments as easily. So when a fast-moving river with lots of sediments in it slows down, the sediments start to sink to the bottom of the river. Over time, slow rivers will drop lots of sediments, and eventually all those sediments can actually start to block the river! That makes the river flow around the sediments that it has dropped. But it will start to leave sediments along its new path, too. Eventually, after a long time and after the river has changed its path again and again, all of those sediments will make a broad, flat area that becomes a plain.

Plains are often home to lots of grasses and grazing animals. They usually have only small hills and few trees, so they make good farming land.

A similar kind of plain can form around rivers when they flood. When too much water tries to go into a river all at once, the river can spill over and flood the area around it. Floods like this make flat plains on either side of the river called **floodplains**.

This river has flooded into its floodplain. Can you see the winding path of the river? Now look at how much water has spilled out into the flat areas around it.

The Great Plains make up a large part of central Canada and the United States and started to form when an ancient sea dried up and left behind lots of flat sediments. The Great Plains are found on the edge of the Rocky Mountains.

Plains can also be formed when a sea dries up. Many small seas have flat bottoms, so when the water in them dries up or flows away, a big flat area will be left behind. Much of the Great Plains in the center of the United States and Canada began to form when an ancient sea dried up!

DESERTS

A **desert** is a very dry region where there is very little rain and few plants. Deserts can form in a few different ways, but many form near mountain ranges because the mountains can block rainclouds from getting to the desert. For example, if rain clouds above a warm ocean blow toward mountains, the mountains will cause the clouds to try to rise over them. But it is cold at the tops of mountains, and the cold air causes the rain clouds to drop their water as rain and snow on the side of the mountain that faces the ocean where the clouds came from. That means that the other side of the mountains, farther from the ocean, don't get any of the rain! This is called a **rain shadow**, and the dry side of the mountain can become a hot, dusty desert with very few plants.

A rain shadow happens when tall, cold mountains cause clouds blowing in from an ocean to drop their rain on the ocean side, leaving a "shadow" of dryness on the far side of the mountain where a desert can then form.

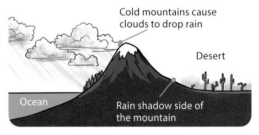

Cold mountains cause clouds to drop rain

Desert

Ocean

Rain shadow side of the mountain

Rainforests are wet, lush forests that are home to countless plants and animals, some of which are found nowhere else on Earth! Rainforests are not formed by rock formations, but the shape of landforms in the region can help keep the forests very wet.

RAINFORESTS

A **rainforest** is a very wet forest that sees a lot of rainfall and has incredible amounts of trees and other plant life. While rock formations do not cause rainforests to develop, they can help. Many rainforests are found in huge basins (remember, a basin is a bowl-shaped low spot) which help hold water and keep them very wet. Some rainforests may have nearby mountains that help keep the rain clouds from blowing away, and water flowing down the mountains washes into the forest.

RIVERS, DELTAS, AND ALLUVIAL FANS

Rivers are a big part of the water cycle, and you've probably seen rivers with different shapes. That's because the speed of the river can change what it looks like. Rivers that are pretty straight are ones that are flowing very quickly, and they cause a lot of erosion. Winding, curving rivers are ones that are flowing slowly, and they often drop their sediments because they aren't flowing fast enough to carry it any farther.

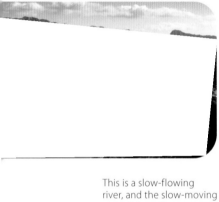

This river is flowing down from the mountains in the background. It is a fast-flowing river. You can tell by how straight it is.

This is a slow-flowing river, and the slow-moving water takes a longer path by winding and curving around.

Even the fastest-flowing rivers slow down when they reach a lake or an ocean. A river often gets much slower and spreads out wider in the place where it meets a larger body of water. This makes an area of mud and sand shaped like a paper fan. This is called a

The area inside the dotted white line is a river delta. See how the river splits up into smaller rivers before it meets the lake?

delta. In a delta, the river often splits up into many smaller rivers before they flow into the lake or ocean.

much sediment
and clay build u

Lastly, some rivers, including ones that have dried up, carry so much sediment that it all piles up in a cone- or pyramid-shaped pile called an **alluvial fan** *(say it "ah-loo-vee-al fan")*. That's a scientific term for it, but it isn't complicated: it is a landform made up of all the sediment a river has dumped out of it.

The area inside the dotted white line is an alluvial fan. It's a huge, wide pyramid-shaped pile of sand and gravel that formed when rivers flowing out of the mountains dropped sediments. There's no river there now, but we know from the alluvial fan that powerful rivers do appear when it rains in the mountains!

167

CAVES, SINKHOLES, AND KARST

Sometimes underground water can have acids in it that can weather and erode certain kinds of rocks. Limestone is a type of sedimentary rock that will dissolve and wash away in acids. So when a lot of acidic groundwater washes through limestone, parts of the rock wash away with it, and amazing landforms like caves and sinkholes can appear!

Karst is a type of texture that limestone gets when it has been weathered on the surface. It has lots of cracks and grooves in it.

A **cave** is an opening underground. Many caves have interesting rock formations inside them, including **stalactites**, which are cone-shaped rocks that hang down from the ceiling, and **stalagmites**, which are cone-shaped rocks that rise up from the floor. Groundwater can make caves larger, weakening the ground above them. If the ground above a cave becomes too thin, it will collapse and fall in, making a big hole called a **sinkhole**.

When limestone is the top layer of rock on the Earth's surface, water can weather it there, too. Rain will quickly weather limestone and give it a unique texture full of lots of cracks and grooves. This type of texture is called **karst**, and it can mean that there are caves or sinkholes in the area!

Sinkholes happen when groundwater has dissolved and washed away so much limestone underground that the surface becomes weak. Eventually, the surface can fall in and form a deep hole. Sometimes sinkholes have water at the bottom.

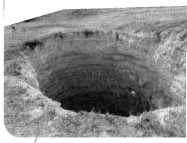

In karst, lots of cracks can open up in the rock, which let rainwater flow down into it. All that water weathers the limestone even more.

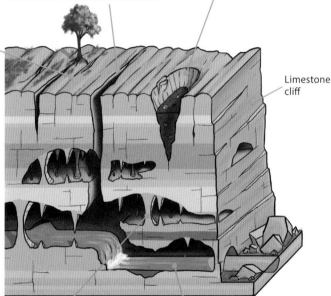

Limestone cliff

In areas with lots of groundwater, whole underground rivers can form! They can wash away lots of limestone, causing many caves and sinkholes to appear.

Deep inside limestone formations, caves can form. Caves happen when groundwater dissolves and washes away lots of limestone, leaving open areas inside. Caves can have stalactites, which hang from the roof, and stalagmites, which rise from the floor, and when they meet in the middle, they form a solid column. They form when water with minerals in it drips from the roof.

Sugary Caves and Karst

Rock textures like karst and landforms like caves and sinkholes all form because limestone can be dissolved, or washed away, by water (especially acidic water). You can get an idea of how water can affect limestone at home by using sugar cubes, which also dissolve in water (but much more quickly than limestone!). You'll need a big jar, some clay, some warm water, a straw or eyedropper, and plenty of sugar cubes. Then, try this:

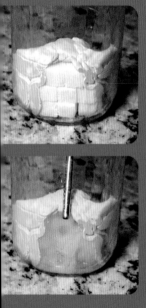

Stack some sugar cubes in the bottom of a jar, against the glass where you can see them. Then pack some clay tightly around the sugar cubes to lock them in place. Put clay on all sides of the sugar cubes except for an opening at the top. In this activity, the sugar cubes represent limestone, and the clay represents other kinds of rocks that don't dissolve easily in water.

Then take a straw, eyedropper, or even a spoon, and carefully drip water onto the top of the sugar cubes. Do it slowly and just a few drops at a time. Watch what happens. You'll see the water begin to dissolve the sugar cubes and make them fall. This is a lot like how acidic water in the ground can dissolve limestone and make it collapse.